To Christian —

Always dare to dream big and reach high.

Merry Christmas

Gary Steen

2007

SONG OF BERNADETTE

A Mother's Memoir of a Daughter

DEBRA S. LEWIS

Bloomington, IN  Milton Keynes, UK

AuthorHouse™
1663 Liberty Drive, Suite 200
Bloomington, IN 47403
www.authorhouse.com
Phone: 1-800-839-8640

AuthorHouse™ UK Ltd.
500 Avebury Boulevard
Central Milton Keynes, MK9 2BE
www.authorhouse.co.uk
Phone: 08001974150

© 2007 Debra S. Lewis. All rights reserved.

No part of this book may be reproduced, stored in a retrieval system, or transmitted by any means without the written permission of the author.

First published by AuthorHouse 7/16/2007

ISBN: 978-1-4259-9508-9 (sc)
ISBN: 978-1-4259-9509-6 (hc)

Library of Congress Control Number: 2007903783

Printed in the United States of America
Bloomington, Indiana

This book is printed on acid-free paper.

In Loving Memory of Bernadette Celeste Lewis

1973-1999

SONG OF BERNADETTE

there was a child named Bernadette
I heard the story long ago
she saw the queen of heaven once
and kept the vision in her soul

no one believed what she had heard
that there were sorrows to be healed
and mercy, mercy in this world

so many hearts I find
broke like yours and mine
torn by what we've done and can't undo
I just want to hold you
won't you let me hold you
like Bernadette would do

tonight, tonight I cannot rest
I've got this joy here in my breast
to think that I did not forget
that child, that song of Bernadette

"Song of Bernadette" ©1980 by
Jennifer Warnes, Leonard and William Elliott

WORDS ARE LIKE PRESERVATIVES

They preserve meaning long after meaning has been lost; a poem, a love letter, the Gettysburg Address are all examples. The meaning we derive now is in actuality from the past. What present importance we will capture in words for the future has yet to be determined. Therefore, nothing we do now really means anything.

7/18/93 Bernadette Lewis (Age 20 years)

I want to be a writer. But sometimes I wonder if I'm the only one who would read my writing. I don't want to have to explain my words or their meaning. I judge that writers are forced to prove that their ideas are interesting. I can't decide whether I want to write fiction or nonfiction. Probably the former, as no one would otherwise believe me.

10/07/95 (Age 22 years)

Prologue: Song Of Bernadette

"The Song of Bernadette" is a tune that I first heard when Bernadette Celeste Lewis was placed into my arms in the early morning hours of Thursday, March 15, 1973. It is a melody that whispered into my ear during the anguished first days following Sunday, October 24, 1999, when my daughter, "Berni," passed on to her next life at age twenty-six years. In between, the song went on, sometimes haltingly, usually passionately, and always genuinely. It is a harmony whose echoes help give me the courage to survive her passing.

I am a good person. I don't know why losing my daughter at such a young age happened to me. Like so many things in life, it just wasn't fair. What happened to me was beyond my control. Since then, my life has gone on.

Bernadette's song is filled with innocence, love, courage, humor, and deep compassion. It is also filled with conflict, tension, loneliness, insecurity, and self-doubt. Bernadette's song is harmonious and memorable, despite not having as many verses as others with more years.

It has been several years since Bernadette passed over to her new life. I received the inspiration to write this memoir on the day of her second funeral service, held on October 31, 1999, in Washburn, Wisconsin.

In the years since her passing, I have tried to gather together the notes in order to hear more clearly the full melody of Bernadette's song. Fortunately for me, Bernadette left behind a rich legacy in her writing.

This is a collection of writing honoring and celebrating the life of "my Berni," pieced together in her own words. I have had the pleasure of reading through all that has been made available to me: scraps, lists, letters, journals, poems, and essays. I have selected and organized those writings that appear to me to most accurately reflect the remarkable and complex young woman I know as my daughter.

For several reasons, I have woven the tale of Berni's life through my eyes as her mother who loved her. First and most selfishly, the process of writing this book has served as a vehicle for my grief process following the terrible loss of my daughter. In the intervening years, this labor of love has gone forward in fits and starts. The process remained stuck for about two years until I was led to realize the time was finally right for releasing Bernadette's story and song and sharing it with others, rather than holding it so close to my heart. Finally, I have been able to bring forth the product of the seeds that were sown so many years ago.

I have decided to share this work with the world because there are many who knew my daughter. I want to share these precious glimpses into her spirit as a special remembrance for those who were touched by Berni's life—and death at such a young age. We who love her grieve her passing from this life. We struggle to celebrate her victory over death as we try to imagine her new more perfect creation and form. Like the psalmist in Psalm 27, "I would have lost heart, unless I had believed that I would see the goodness of God in the land of the living."

I have also decided to share this story for those who never knew my daughter. There are others who walk this journey that I have, who have experienced a loss so devastating that hopelessness has threatened the ability to continue. This book is my attempt to open the door to an alternative to hopelessness and to share the tools that have worked for me in my process, in the belief that they might be of some use to others still struggling not to lose heart.

Losing a child, for me, was like being shattered to pieces. It was excruciatingly painful, both physically and emotionally. I have never had abdominal surgery, but I liken the pain in the first year to what I have been told is common for those whose insides have been cut. At times, the physical agony I felt was worse than the labor of childbirth. It was unrelenting. At first, I had no appetite for days. The food I ate seemed to run through me, and I lost weight at an alarming rate. I was barely able to get out of bed in the morning, and there were many days when I didn't at first.

My grief process started with an intense disbelief as I heard the words from the police officer: "Your daughter in Baltimore ... is dead ... trying to jump onto a moving train." The words had no meaning, because at that moment I could not imagine my daughter in Baltimore trying to jump onto a moving train.

"You have made a mistake." I thought. "My daughter is cautious and afraid of things like that."

Later that night, after the long-distance calls to the Baltimore Police Department and the coroner confirmed my worst fears, the reality began to sink in. I collapsed into the arms of my beloved husband and cried the rest of the night. When I arrived in Baltimore the next morning, after an early-morning cross-country plane ride, my eyes were so swollen shut and my body so exhausted from crying that I had to purchase sunglasses and lean on my husband because I could barely stand.

When we arrived in Baltimore, it was a beautiful, sunny autumn day. The fall foliage was at the peak of its splendor. Looking back, the splendor of the day after learning the news that would change my world forever was a gift that started the process of my rebuilding the shattered pieces of my life.

Now, seven years later, others have observed that I have healed well from the nightmare of this experience. I agree with them. I get up each day and go to work. I am productive and competent in my professional work. I enjoy my life and find profound meaning in the gift of each day. I am happier and more at peace now than I have ever been. I am optimistic about the future.

How did I get from there to here? How have I managed to go on with my life without bitterness and experience enough healing to enable me to not only function in my life, but to be transformed? These are the questions I reflected on as I attempted in this work to share what helped me.

The writings fell naturally into an order connected to the seasons: "spring" was the era from birth to approximately high school; "summer" was the season of high school and my daughter's college career; "autumn" was post-college and professional years; and "winter" was associated with Bernadette's writings at the end of her earthly life and her thoughts about death, afterlife, and immortality.

I do not pretend that this selection is a comprehensive collection showing all of Bernadette's many facets: That is an impossible task. I have meant only to provide glimpses of her spirit. I continue to hear additional musical notes and phrases as they occasionally break through the stilting silence of her death, at times drowning out the gentle groanings of grief. I remind myself that I am not the composer. I want Bernadette's words to speak for themselves, and I have therefore chosen to editorialize her writing only where I think it necessary to add context for the reader. It is my hope that by reading firsthand about the inner struggles of one life, you, the reader, can recognize a central truth: That no matter what we do or how long we live, every one of us on earth plays a central role in the history of the world. Most of us don't even know it.

Bernadette has been transformed by her passage into a new creation, as have we who love her. I am not the same person I was before. That person died with my daughter. I am better than before. The great paradox of this experience is that it is both the worst thing that ever happened to me and the best thing. When I write these words, I think about the concept of agony and ecstasy together. Two sides of the coin. Sorrow and joy intermixed. I have felt both sides with great intensity. Neither alone defines the experience, nor does it define me. But together, the sorrow and the joy have transformed me and imbued me with more courage than I ever dreamed of in facing the challenges of life. When the worst has already happened to you and you survive, other challenges that come along pale in comparison.

The visual eludes. But I hear Berni's music in her words, and in the words of those who knew her and loved her, and in the things she made and wore and did. If I listen carefully, I can hear her song playing in the distance.

"The Song of Bernadette" calls to me like a siren song: rhapsodizing, haunting, delighting, and warming. It is complete and perfect and whole. It touches my soul and inspires me. I want to turn up the volume.

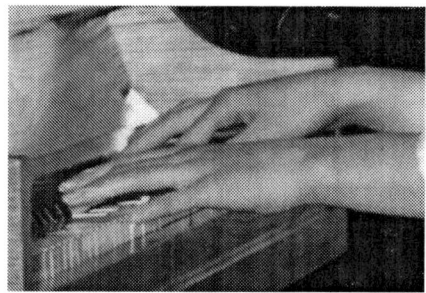

Table of Contents

Prologue: Song Of Bernadette..xi

Book One: Seasons 1

I. Spring 3

Ii. Summer..39

Iii. Autumn...81

Iv. Winter...101

Epilogue: Song Of Bernadette...127

Book Two: Choices..129

Chapter 1 131

Chapter 2 133

Chapter 3 135

Chapter 4 137

Chapter 5 141

Chapter 6 143

Chapter 7 147

Chapter 8 149

Chapter 9 151

Chapter 10 153

AFTERWORD 157

ACKNOWLEDGMENTS 163

Book One:

Seasons

I. SPRING

First Day Of Spring:

Wake Up!
And End Your Rest
The Time Has Come-
The Time That's Best

A Time Anew
To Try Again
To Pray For Sun
To Hope For Rain

So Life Enhanced
Can Come To Life
And Learn Again
Learn To Like

To Like What's Right
What God Has Made
Like Its Beauty
Before It Fades.

3/20/91 (Age 18 Years)

Debra S. Lewis

SPRING

Spring is a favorite time of year for many of us. It is a welcome season of hope after the long dark days of winter. For us northerners, it is our gift for enduring the winters in our lives. Spring is fresh and young and rejuvenating, a time when all things are made new. It is a time of coming out into the world and stretching toward the longer hours of sunlight. It is a time of being planted and refreshed by the rains.

Bernadette Celeste Bauer was born in the spring of 1973, at 7:13 AM on a sunny Thursday, Ides of March morning; first-born child to her eighteen-year-old mother and twenty-year-old father. It was the dawn of the cynical post-Watergate period, just five months before Richard Nixon resigned as president of the United States.

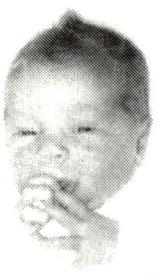

Her first name was chosen and insisted upon by her biological father, who picked it from an old song he had heard and liked. Despite protestations to the contrary, her birth father decided that even with such a long name, no one would ever refer to this daughter as "Berni." I, as her mother, knew intuitively that the nickname "Berni" would be impossible to avoid once she entered school. I chose and favored her second name, Celeste, a name picked from my high school yearbook, and one that spoke of my heavenly dreams for my daughter. During Bernadette's earliest years, she was addressed randomly by her middle name, which never gained widespread acceptance by friends and family. By the time she entered school, she was Bernadette.

As a young child, Bernadette was bright, calm, and agreeable.

Bernadette was fortunate to have my full-time care and attention for her first several years. She was unfortunate to witness her mother during this time in an abusive relationship. When she was nearly four years old, Bernadette stood, terror-stricken and barefoot, in the fading snows of winter late at night, where she had run across the street following my screams and witnessed her father bashing my head on the neighbor's sidewalk. Soon thereafter, her birth parents split up for good. I fled the marriage in order to survive, taking Bernadette and her one-year-old sister, Jenine, to live in the first of several apartments.

We three women—two young girls and a young single mother—became a close-knit unit, woven together by the certainty of each other's presence during the times of great financial uncertainty that followed the divorce.

I went to school soon after the divorce and became a licensed practical nurse. Bernadette started school in Robbinsdale, Minnesota, and soon became an academic standout.

In 1982, when Berni was nine years old, her future course was changed dramatically. I met and fell in love with Jeffrey Lewis, a young, first-year family-practice resident, and married him in 1984. In order to repay a National Health Service obligation, Jeff was required to commit four years of medical practice to an underserved community in need of medical care. The year 1985 was important in Bernadette's twelve-year-old life. In May of that year, with the consent of her biological father, she and her sister, Jenine, were adopted by Jeff Lewis. The re-formed family moved in June 1985 to Kenton, Ohio, a rural, medically underserved community of 8,000 people.

Bernadette's coming-of-age years in Kenton were notable in several respects. She remained an academic standout in school, and had one best friend, Melissa Taylor. It was a time of great innocence and simplicity.

Summers were spent lounging near or in the three-acre pond adjacent to the 120-year-old brick farmhouse in which we lived, or at the seashore home of her paternal grandparents in New Jersey.

Bernadette was born with a jaw malformation which needed to be corrected surgically during her high school years. When she was in tenth grade, she had extensive facial surgery, involving the installation of metal plates in her jaw. The surgery required an overnight ICU stay and her jaw to be wired shut for several weeks afterward.

During these years, Bernadette fell in love with horses and persuaded her city-slicker parents to purchase a Morgan mare as a 4-H project. She studied the fine arts of dressage and showed "Star" at a few county fair shows, before tiring of the work involved in caring for a horse. She studied dance and she learned to play the piano.

Bernadette was a late bloomer socially. She began to come into her own during her later high school years. Always the idealist and the sentimentalist, she loved seeing relatives and relished family holidays together, especially Christmas.

Debra S. Lewis

A DAY IN THE LIFE OF BERNADETTE BAUER

When I first get up, I rub my eyes to make sure I'm awake. Listen to my radio or watch T.V. Get dressed. Wait 'til my mom comes home from work then she makes breakfast then we eat breakfast. Get ready to go to school, get my coat on, go to the bus stop, wait for the bus. At school, we wait until the bell rings. Teacher does the attendance sheet. Do work. Go to recess. Come in. Finish our work. Play for about an whole hour. Get our lunch tickets. Go out for recess. Come in; eat lunch. Our teacher picks up, up we go to our room, and do an art project until recess. Come in from recess, do math. Go home. I take the bus home, have a snack at home, listen to my radio, watch t.v., eat supper, play, or watch t.v., and go to bed.

March 9, 1981 (Age 8 years)

WHEN I BECAME SHY

I don't imagine that I was born shy, although it is often argued that genetics, rather than social experiences, separate the introverted from the extroverts. So maybe I wasn't born carefree. As the oldest daughter of four, perhaps I possess a "natural" sense of responsibility. But I don't accept genetics as an explanation for most of my shyness, for my sensitivity or my self consciousness when meeting new people. There has to be some greater force which causes my reticence to run so deep.

(Undated Journal Entry)

Debra S. Lewis

MUSIC

*I love to hear the trumpet play,
I love to hear music every day.
The piano is what I like best.
When you're done playing it,
You can take a rest.*

*I like to dance,
And it's fun to prance.
I like to dance from room to room
Zoom, Zoom, Zoom, Boom, Boom, Boom,
From room to room.*

1983 (age 10 years)

Song of Bernadette

FAITH

*Faith is important in life,
You wouldn't be able to live without it.
Because it is a wonderful feeling
The feeling that seems to fit.*

*Faith/Love
Put them together and you have a puzzle.*

June 8, 1983 (age 10 years)

Debra S. Lewis

STAR'S PLAY

*Run like the wind, Star.
Go wild and free
Just forget where you are
And I'll let you be.*

*Kick up your heels
And jump for joy.
Tell me how it feels
With a snort loud and coy.*

*Round and round and round you go
With tramples so hard they shake the ground
In the breeze your mane and tail both flow
As in circles you run around and around.*

December 1987 (Age 14 years)

ON DANCE

When my parents would go out when I was younger, my sister and I would turn on some music and dance around the living room. We'd put together routines and perform them in front of my parents when they returned home. One evening, my dad asked us if we would like to take lessons. We both replied with an enthusiastic yes. That is how my interest in dance began.

With the many changes in my life, dance has been one of the few things that has remained constant. Within the classroom, I have developed technique, style, and grace. I have learned to value cooperation and persistence.

Dance has taught me how to live better outside the classroom as well. It gives me the confidence to overcome my feelings of inhibition. It has helped me develop a positive attitude and feelings of self-worth.

Dance is not a sport. It is an art. The appreciation of dance is a vital part of my life. To me, dance is not merely a series of steps, but a way of living.

(Undated High School Essay)

Debra S. Lewis

When she was thirteen, my mom's father left home, leaving behind five children and a future generation of pain. It was then that my mom became a mom, though she wouldn't become mine for nearly six more years.

For my thirteenth birthday, I was given a facial and had my nails done in a salon. Afterwards, we went to a fancy Japanese restaurant where the chef cooks your meal at your table. I felt beautiful that night with my new look.

Debra S. Lewis

When Grandpa Paul traded his family for booze, my grandma had to work outside the home. First, she had to learn how to pump gas so that she could get to work. My mom, as the oldest daughter, learned to cook, clean, and do laundry.

My sister and I used to hate having to do the dishes. Before the "chore wheel" was developed, we'd do the dishes together. Sometimes it took us hours. We'd fill one sink full of bubbles, wash one dish at a time and, after rinsing, use them to build "castles" in the second sink.

By the time she was seventeen, my mom was really sick of doing dishes. That's when she married her first boyfriend. She soon found out that cleaning was a much easier task than maintaining a marriage. Still, she tried for five years. Her greatest accomplishments, from those years, she used to say, were the births of her two girls.

My mom always used to tell me to make decisions for myself; to do what was right for me. She told me not to sacrifice my own desires because of someone else—in particular, because of a man. My first serious boyfriend and I went to college in separate states. He married someone else.

After my mom's divorce, she waitressed for a little while, then became a nurse. As a nurse, she learned how to french braid hair and I used to love it when she practiced on me. My sister and I went to the babysitter's during the day, and sometimes went to sleep there. Vivid in my memory is one night when I happened to be sick. My mom came to pick us up and bring us home, carrying

*us to the car over her shoulders. I threw up
and was hot. She sang me to sleep.*

(Undated Essay)

BEING ALONE IN A CROWD

Forms of alienation, "a withdrawing or separation of a person and his family from the values and positions of a society," have been felt by too many throughout history. During World War II, Hitler persecuted Jews with unbelievable malice and hostility just because they were Jewish. Even though one would think things would change over the years, they haven't.

Gays and lesbians are not readily accepted in today's society just because of their sexual preference. Democracy-seeking Chinese were persecuted in Beijing merely for their political views. The list of injustices done to minority groups is long and unfortunate.

I, too, have felt alienated, however, the feeling was temporary. I moved to Kenton from Minnesota when I was twelve. I came from a home in the suburbs of Minneapolis, a large city in comparison to Kenton. The change was tremendous, as were the adjustments to be made. I knew nobody when I started seventh grade, even though everyone else seemed to know everybody. Eventually, I met people and the feeling of alienation subsided.

Still, we are all put in situations at one time or another where we don't know anyone. I think it is good to be able to learn to deal with that feeling.

November 3, 1987 (Age 14 years)

Song of Bernadette

LETTER HOME FROM SHORE

*Hello, Mother, Hello, Father,
Life here is great at the shore.
How's the house coming in Ohio?
Have you heard much from Mark and Cindy?*

*We received a letter from Carrie today!
Also I got a new bathing suit from Grancy.
How's the pets? And the cats?
Can't wait to see you but I don't want to leave yet.
When does school start for sure?
Guess what? Ziggy went in the ocean for the first time.
It was funny!
I'll tell you more about it when we get back. I've been
reminded to write this letter all day and decided to at
9:15 PM. Well, hope you enjoyed.
Miss you both lots!!*

Love, Berni

July 26, 1985 (Age 12 years)

Debra S. Lewis

LETTER HOME (SUMMER 1986)

DEAR MOM, DAD, LUTIE, TATTI

Been eating food that's really fatty.
Water's pretty fresh
Baby keeps making mess. (Sort-of-rhyme)
How's Ohio weather?
Here it's as hot as a feather?!?!?!
Wrote to Karen a nice, long letter,
So thought the same to you I better.
Thought rhyme was an interesting twist
To tell you just how much you are missed.
Love you much and much and much
(By the way) but some stuff and other such.
I'll write again soon
When I'm not in the mood of a goon.
Love ya lots,
Berni is tops

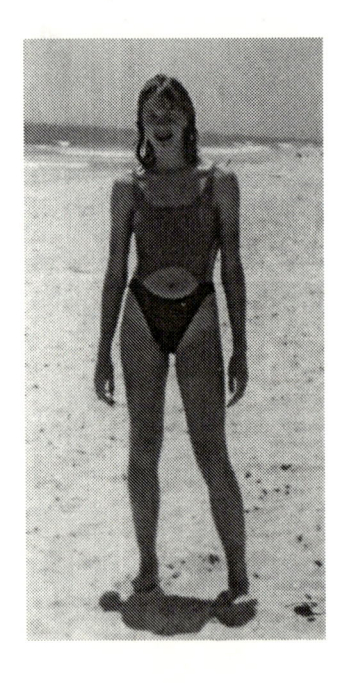

ON GOLDEN POND

After school lets out and summer vacation has started, everyone is posed with the problem of keeping busy. Many take trips, whether it be to the beach, to visit relatives, or to camp. I'd like to tell you about my favorite vacation at Rockywold-Deephaven Camp. This vacation was the most memorable because of the location, the people I was with, and the activities I was doing.

Rockywold-Deephaven Camp is located in New Hampshire on Squam Lake. Squam Lake is shallow with many rocks jutting out over the water's surface. It has many islands and is surrounded by the White Mountains. This is the same place where the movie, On Golden Pond, was filmed and I have been past the dock that Jane Fonda did her famous backflip off. The woodsy land, the reflecting waters with the call of a loon in the distance, and the mountains, make Squam the ideal setting for a two-week vacation.

I was not only in the perfect place, but I was with the people I cared most about— my family. My parents, my grandparents, my sister and I all stayed in a two-story, five- bedroom cabin called Cliffside. Cliffside was located on large boulders that blended together and steeply ran down to the water's edge.

Debra S. Lewis

This vacation is one time I can remember that everyone got along. It is also one of the few times that my grandpa and I talked. The staff at the camp also made the trip enjoyable. There were maids to make the beds and clean up the cabin. There were chefs who prepared wonderful meals. The trip allowed me to escape work and responsibility and placed emphasis on relaxation.

The camp staff provided entertainment as well. There was capture the flag and square dancing for all ages. We brought a canoe and laser sailboat and enjoyed sailing in the afternoons. I also climbed my first mountains at Squam. There were many things to do, either planned or at one's leisure.

Squam Lake is the type of place that no one wants to leave.
1986(Age 13 years)

Song of Bernadette

Debra S. Lewis

CHRISTMAS MEANS TO ME....

FUN

One of our Christmas traditions is to go to Grandma and Grandpa's house either on Christmas Eve or Christmas Day.

Over there, we have a big celebration with my aunts, uncles, my great-grandma Irene, and my cousins. We all have lots of fun. When we first get there, Grandma is usually making dinner.

Before dinner, we all talk in the living room or watch TV or play games. To make everything more cheerful, someone will put on a record. That puts everybody in a good mood for dinner.

When Grandma cooks, she cooks. Mainly we have potatoes and gravy, some sort of meat like turkey or ham, potato or other soup, lutafisk (which isn't my favorite), a vegetable, pie, cake, or both, and cookies.

After our feast, we load her dishwasher and go into the living room to settle our stomachs. When our stomachs are settled, we open presents. There are many presents under the tree to be opened. After they are opened, we all pitch in to clean up.

This year, I have no idea what I'm doing for Christmas. It will be our last *year here (in Minneapolis) and Jeff and my mom work.*

What Christmas means to me is this: The joy of being together with my family to celebrate.

(1984) age 11 years

Debra S. Lewis

MEMORIES OF CHRISTMAS...

by Bernadette Lewis in the year of 1985

I've always thought of Christmas as togetherness with family or happiness with friends. A time for fun. A time for sharing and giving. A time when there is laughter.

In my memories, all those things are there. The spirit of Christmas is always in our hearts and minds.

I can remember Christmas where I got my favorite outfit or a brand new sled. But those things are just there. I mean, what's special about that? What's special is that Christmas always turned out with happiness. That no matter what, Christmas was looked forward to.

I guess I've kind of come off my topic (which I have a tendency to do when I write), but what I'm trying to say is that I don't remember Christmas for what I get as gifts, but for who's there and the fun we have together.

(Age 12 years)

Song of Bernadette

Debra S. Lewis

CHRISTMAS OF 1986

This Christmas shall be far different than last year's, and probably the years before that.

First of all, it is the first Christmas that I can remember in which we've had no snow. It just doesn't seem like Christmas. It's supposed to be white—I never dreamed of a green Christmas! But it actually is. The only proof of winter is the bareness of the trees and maybe the calendar's pages opened to December.

Second of all, and a more happy prospect is the new puppy, Maggie. We will have had her almost a week on Christmas Day. I can picture the wrapping paper and her. The combination means mischief will be coming our way. But, oh what a way to celebrate the love and happiness she's brought.

The other Christmas traditions stand as normal: Gingerbread men and women, rum-pum-pum-pum, the blinking lights and presents that go with the 8 foot tall tree, to name just a few. They all spell out one thing, with or without snow and puppies: they are things that mean CHRISTMAS.

December 21, 1986 (Age 13 years)

Song of Bernadette

Debra S. Lewis

BERNI'S CHRISTMAS LIST (1988)

1/ Keyboard

2/ Cordless curling iron or Z-curler (flat shaped)

3/ Shower radio

4/ Diary

5/ Perfume (Halston)

6/ Tapes (Bangles, Bobby Brown, Susy and the Banjies, Robert Palmer, U2)

Song of Bernadette

7/ Earrings/bracelets

8/ Bikini underwear

9/ Scruples

10/ Socks and turtlenecks

11/ Piano music (books or sheets)

12/ Sweatshirts (Benneton, Esprit, Guess, Yale University, Don't be a Dick-the drink, drive, die one)

13/ Sweaters (oversized cardigan or cables, red preferred)

14/ Hair accessories

15/ Pants (casual, somewhat baggy, pair of light blue guess jeans)

16/ Dancewear

(Age 15 years)

Debra S. Lewis

MY PAST, PRESENT AND FUTURE

My mom ran away from home and was married in Tijuana, Mexico when she was seventeen. She had me when she was nearly nineteen. My mom's marriage to my dad was brief. She was divorced and had two kids by the age of twenty-one. About ten years later, she married Jeff Lewis. He adopted my sister and me, and I consider him to be my dad. I see my biological father once a year and correspond with him infrequently.

I can think of three major changes in my life. One is the birth of my sister, Jenine Nicole (1975). I was two and a half years old when she was born. We used to fight, but now we are very close.

The second change occurred in 1985. The government paid for my dad's medical school. In return, he had to work where there was a shortage of doctors. Forest, Ohio qualified, and so we moved to Kenton, Ohio, the biggest town nearby. It was a big change to come from a suburb of Minneapolis, Minnesota to a small country town in the middle of nowhere. It took a lot of adjusting and adopting to my whole new way of life.

The last big change in my life happened recently when another sister was born on November 5, 1988. Her name is Emily Jefferys. Babysitting for a few hours is definitely not the same as living full-time with a baby.

Although all my changes have disadvantages, they are all for the better. I'm glad both my sisters were born, and I suppose I was destined to live in Kenton.

I have many interests, talents, and goals. I like to dance. I've taken lessons for five years. I also play the piano. I have a Morgan mare which I enjoy riding. I'm a member of the Hardin County Joy Riders 4-H club. I'm also a member of Student Senate, S.A.D.D., and Quiz Bowl.

One goal I have in life is to join the Peace Corps. I think it would be a very fun and exciting to make a difference by helping others. Something else I would like to do is to travel to Europe. It is one of my biggest dreams. I have never been outside the United States. I would like to have a real experience with another culture, a foreign language, and different people. Having a Japanese exchange student stay with us has helped me realize how much this dream means to me.

Family is important to me. I like the love that develops between each family member in my family of origin. However, having my own family does not take top priority in my future. My education and career come first.

Debra S. Lewis

In college, I would like to major in either biological sciences or psychology.
After college, I will need to attend medical school for my career.

December 1988 (Age 15 years)

Song of Bernadette

AS ONE CAN SEE'

As one can see
A fly, an ant, a snail, a bee
A monkey, a lion, a turtle, a flea.

As one can be
A lawyer, a veterinarian, a doctor
Or even lots more,
Or maybe, just be a jock on the shore.

1984 (Age 11 years)

II. SUMMER

THE START

Early morning
Sun is Rising
Birds are singing
Their own song

Time is passing
Life is happenin'
New adventures
On the way

Debra S. Lewis

*Day is Forming
New Beginnings
Everywhere and every
Way it's here*

*Live it freely
Happily too
Each day and new
Beginning*

1985 (Age 12 years)

Song of Bernadette

THE KIND OLD MAN

She was walking along the cool sand
The chilly water against bare toes
A kite steals her attention
The urge to fly comes
A man flying the kite she nears
For a brief moment she stands close to him
The kind one handed her the wooden bar
She felt she was in control of the sky
She handed it back and left

1985 (Age 12 years)

Debra S. Lewis

FLY AWAY

Sometimes, don't you want to fly away?
Just for a day.
And listen to the lake
Knowing that nature's not a fake.
Watching the growing trees,
Feeling the morning breeze.

Just...Fly Away,
For a day!

1984 (Age 11 years)

A FLIGHT OF GENEROSITY

I jumped a height
of a thousand feet
Flew like a kite
In the summer's heat

Then drifted down
Unto the ground
Into a town
And I looked around

I saw a man
Sitting in a chair.
He was holding a can
And wore flowers in his hair

I dropped a penny
Into the tin
It combined with many
On his face was a grin

I felt proud
To have helped the poor
And I said aloud
"If only I could give you more."

He gave me a humble smile
In this man's own special way
I had flown mile after mile
To make happy this poor man's day.

Debra S. Lewis

SUMMER

Summer is a season of dynamic activity and energy. We wear less clothing, get outdoors more, and generally move more in summer. It is a time of rapid growth and productivity, a time when all growing things are more lush and abundant. It is a warm season, filled with long days of sunshine, water sports, and insects. I tend to partake in more adventures and take more risks in summer.

As she achieved academic success, Berni began to blossom in her late high school years into a more self-confident, worldly, and insightful person. Despite her outward confidence, there was a part of her deep inside that doubted whether or not she was loveable. She was self-conscious about her appearance. As with most young people, a common theme for her during this time was lamenting over the confusion of the first stirrings of adolescent love, and wondering if she would ever find a "special someone" just for her.

During the summer of 1990, Berni was selected to participate in a science exchange program that enabled her to spend three weeks in the former Soviet Union just prior to the collapse of the communist system there. During her trip, she stayed with a Soviet family and experienced firsthand the disparities between the standard of living in the United States and that of other lesser-developed countries. The trip had a profound impact on her, and thereafter, she developed wanderlust and began to allow herself to dream big about her ability to make a difference in the world.

During the summer following her junior year in high school, Berni began the interviewing process for college. From the beginning of her process, Berni made it clear that she was going to go far. As her middle school principal stated to me after meeting her, "Berni has the ambition of someone who wants to go places. There is no doubt that she will." She applied to Yale—her adoptive father's alma mater—and was disappointed not to be accepted. She was drawn to the East Coast Ivy League setting, despite the personal hardship of moving so far away from her family. After much deliberation, she eventually settled on Mount Holyoke College, a small, private women's college located in South Hadley, Massachusetts.

In June of 1991, Bernadette graduated first in her class at Kenton High School and gave the student commencement address. Her words now do not appear to be particularly profound or noteworthy. The remarkableness of the event was that the girl who started life as a shy self-doubter was able to publicly speak with such poise and confidence. She was starting to come of age.

Debra S. Lewis

In the last week of August 1991, Bernadette and I set out from the farmlands of Kenton, Ohio and headed for a small town in New England in a Chevy van packed to the rafters with most of her earthly possessions. Always a pack rat, Berni found it difficult to part with her possessions. She found it even more difficult to leave family and friends behind. It was a daunting challenge for her to adjust to being in a place of such great distance from the comforts of home. Letters and phone calls during this time were filled with intense longing and expressions of homesickness. At the same time, the experience of being in such a stimulating and supportive intellectual environment for the first time was intoxicating. Very quickly, she awakened to her feminist and politically liberal belief system. She started out her first college year as an international relations major.

During Family Weekend at Mount Holyoke in October 1991, Berni's then-three-year-old sister, Emily and I flew out to see her and stayed in her dorm for the weekend. It was a wonderful time for all three of us. Berni felt a very special bond with Emily, and she loved showing off her little sister to her classmates.

The first year at Mount Holyoke College was a time of great transition for Berni. Never athletic, she stretched her wings and joined a women's rugby team. She tested her limits by exploring a number of diverse extracurricular activities. In time, she settled on biology as her major. This was just the beginning for Bernadette. There was a lot more growth to come.

Debra S. Lewis

IF I COULD CHANGE:

IF I COULD CHANGE ONE THING ABOUT THE WORLD, WHAT?

I would like to change lots of things, but if I could do just one, I'd make the world a more happy place. I'd do so by eliminating all grudges, grievances, and distrust. Not everything would always be fun but people wouldn't complain about it.

IF I COULD CHANGE ONE THING ABOUT MYSELF, WHAT?

I'd change my intolerance. Definitely. It really gets in the way sometimes. There are times when I literally want to go nuts because of something or someone. A lot of times I'm sincere about really not being able to stand something, but other times it's petty and stupid.

Undated High School Journal Entries

MY GOALS:

As a person: I try to be a very open and honest person. I want people to like me for who I am. I know that sounds like a couple of lines from a movie, but it's true. When I was in elementary and middle school, I walked looking down at the floor. I was very shy. I don't know what happened, but I have gained so much confidence over the past few years. I am, in certain situations, still hesitant to be the first to start a conversation, but at least now I don't die trying. I still think one of the best pieces of advice that I've been given and that I've given others, is to hold your head up high and be proud of who you are. I write much better than I talk because I can plan what I want to say.

I'm a nervous speaker and I'd like to strengthen this skill.

1989 (Age 16 years)

Debra S. Lewis

HAPPINESS IS FEELING GOOD ABOUT YOURSELF

Everybody needs to have some joy in their life. The first step in reaching this goal is liking yourself. If you like yourself and believe in yourself, you can achieve whatever it is that you need to be happy. Doing this is not always easy and takes a lot of confidence. If you like yourself, then others will like you. If you like yourself then you are more apt to lead a fulfilled and satisfying life. It's easier to enjoy yourself and others when you are happy. If you feel good about yourself you can accomplish anything.

Undated High School Essay

Song of Bernadette

WHAT DO I LIKE BEST ABOUT MY LIFE? LEAST?

I like best about my life the fact that I can walk and talk and jump and laugh and cry and feel and touch and be and be normally. I'm glad I don't suffer from disease or illness or abuse. What I like least is that I feel like my freedom of being is hindered by a structured society.

Debra S. Lewis

FOR WHAT IN LIFE DO I FEEL MOST GRATEFUL?

I am the most grateful for those I love and those who love me—my family and friends. All the material objects of the world could not compete with that love generated. It is what feeds my soul and keeps me going.

WOULD I RATHER BE HAPPY, BUT SLOW AND UNIMAGINATIVE OR UNHAPPY, BUT CREATIVE?

I would rather be happy than anything else. A few years ago, I would probably have written the opposite. I used to think that all that mattered was being the best. I would stress myself out constantly trying to succeed above everyone else. Recently, I realized that what I was trying to do isn't possible, and is not a worthy goal. I try now to concentrate more on being happy, even if I have to make some sacrifices. If I was suddenly denied the ability to think, I would still have my happiness and that's how I would want it to be.

Undated High School Journal Entries

Debra S. Lewis

Song of Bernadette

LAMENTATIONS ON LOVE:

LOVE CONFUSES

♥

Lying here at night in bed
I can't express what's in my heart,
My body or my head.
I can't even begin to start.

It vibrates slowly up my spine
To the top vertebrae in my neck
My teeth sometimes grit and grind
And I try not to be a nervous wreck.

It's sort of like a quiver
That makes me limp and meek
But of one thing I know I'm sure
It's thoughts of him that make me weak.

He doesn't know I care
He doesn't know I want
Yet I know he's always there
And to tell him I cannot.

What's this feeling that can't be explained
That always makes me feel so strange
Whatever it is, I know I've gained
By knowing the feeling can't be changed.

1986 (Age 13 years)

Debra S. Lewis

I WISH

I wish between us something could be
Something worthwhile that everyone could see
I wish you loved me not her
Maybe you do but I'm not sure
Or maybe I assume too much
Such as me feeling your soft and gentle touch
Or that wishing between us something could be
That instead of her you loved me
I wish that forever you were mine
And like clusters of grapes upon a vine
We'd be together until the end of time
And like this fruit during its prime
Together we'd have things be so sweet
That our oneness could never be beat
Wishful thinking is seldom bad
But mine is discouraging which makes me sad
Because I know right now things will never be
Lovingly special between you and me.

1989 (Age 16 years)

Song of Bernadette

ALWAYS

EVERYWHERE YOU ARE

IS WHERE I WANT TO BE.

EVERYTHING YOU SEE IS WHAT I WANT TO SEE.

IN EVERY SONG, I HEAR YOUR VOICE.

IN EVERY THOUGHT, I FEEL YOUR PRESENCE.

YOUR EYES REVEAL, YOUR SMILE ASSURES,

YOU ARE ALWAYS WITH ME!

3/20/91   (Age 18 years)

Debra S. Lewis

ON THE SOVIET UNION

When most people think of the Soviet Union, they think of a major world power. Yet fewer people know that the Soviet Union is considered to be a third-world country. The government spends so much time funding for defense and space travel, etc. but ignores the fact that the political system is not benefiting the people.

Modern conveniences are not modern, first of all, and second, are rare. Owning one's home is a luxury as is owning a car. Soviets are extremely impressed to hear that students have their own car. It's one of the first questions I was asked. As most of you know, I spent three weeks of my summer in the Soviet Union.

I went with thirty-one other U. S. students as a participant in a science exchange program called "People to People." After a three-day orientation in Washington, D.C., our delegation took a thirteen-hour flight to Moscow for three days of sightseeing in the Soviet capital. Then we travelled to Togliatti, a city about 300 miles east of Moscow, to study its pollution problems.

In Moscow, I was lucky enough to be with a group of twelve People to People students, no adults or anyone who knew Russian, who got lost on Arbat Street, a funky street where street sales are everywhere. While we were waiting to be found, we talked to some Soviet police officers who knew no English, we jokingly tried to ask where the American Embassy was. My friend Chandra even had an Arab man try to buy her. It was so much fun, though.

Staying with host families in Togliatti was the best experience of the trip because we were living Soviet life away from our new American friends. In addition to experiencing Soviet generosity with my host families, strangers on the street were friendly and generous, too. Young Soviet girls gave one of our group a large bag of strawberries at a craft fair. Strawberries cost $50 a pint on Moscow streets. The people were friendly and so giving and generous, but there are so many things we have that they don't. It makes me appreciate what I have, but it makes American people look selfish.

Togliatti is home of the largest automobile manufacturer in the Soviet Union. Sixty to eighty percent of Soviet cars are made there. There are sections of Togliatti where twenty-year-old buildings are covered with soot from the auto plant. On a tour of the plant, I learned that the manufacturer recycles its paint. Yet, recycling is uncommon in the Soviet Union because of a lack of recycling centers and environmental groups. Waste from the Togliatti industrial plants and runoff from Chiguli Mountains drains into the Volga River, one of the most polluted rivers in the world.

Debra S. Lewis

Although we were advised against swimming in the Volga, I waded in the water because I did not want to be impolite when my host family invited me in for a swim.

The Soviets were curious about American dancing. We taught the Soviets staying near us in Togliatti how to dance uninhibitedly. We danced to both Soviet and American music. On the Fourth of July, Soviet ten-year-olds serenaded our delegation with American songs.

Last, we toured Leningrad for three days. Leningrad was cold! The water was worse there. Leningrad is in the only place in the Soviet Union where the water is undrinkable.

The food was not much more appetizing than the water. The food was one of the worst experiences. Many in the group became vegetarians during the trip because cow's tongue or monkey did not sound appetizing for breakfast.

Fortunately, I had the opportunity to be in the Soviet Union right before the downfall that is happening now. Unfortunately, I returned two weeks before the Black Market became legal. It used to be illegal to buy things with cash although that was what most sellers on the street wanted. We paid cash anyway but had to do so discreetly. The Black Market sellers were everywhere, identifiable by the fact *that they spoke perfect English and wore American clothes.*

My first trip beyond the U. S. border broadened my perspective of the world. I learned that not everything is like it is in Kenton, Ohio.

1990 (Age 17 years)

Debra S. Lewis

A VALUABLE EVALUATION

During the summer, I faced what many seniors go through and what most dread: college interviews. As I was returning from the Soviet Union to New York, and since I was planning to apply to schools in the east, for convenience, I did some of my college interviews early. To add to the trauma of being "ripped apart" by college judges, I traveled between each college by myself and stayed in hotels, with relatives, and with friends of friends that were acquaintances of my parents.

My first interview was with Bryn Maur, an elite, all-female school known for its high academic standing. Sitting in the waiting room before my name was called, I doubted the originality of my credentials. Finally, my name was called. Only when the interviewer smiled and introduced herself did I begin to feel a little less alienated. I didn't know a tremendous amount about the school, so I had to rely on my personal accomplishments to impress my interviewer. I knew I wanted to portray myself in a positive way without sounding snobby or like a country hick.

Needless to say, the interview went well.

In my four following interviews, the tension beforehand decreased, as did the need for much conversation before I began to become comfortable. I was able to express *myself better and became increasingly confident of my talents.*

Now I can say that I'm glad I was able to do my interviewing early. I no longer have to worry about "quiz" questions or whether or not my qualifications are good enough. It's a satisfying feeling to have lived through interviews. Still, there is a curiosity within me that wonders how I was perceived. Guess I'll find out in April.

1990 (Age 17 years)

Debra S. Lewis

HIGH SCHOOL COMMENCEMENT ADDRESS:

Instead of seeing graduation as the end of anything, let us look at it as the beginning of everything. The years leading us up to this day serve merely as preparation for what we will do the rest of our lives. We are now ready for the final leap into adulthood. As adults, we must learn to rely on ourselves and our abilities. For the past thirteen years, education has been our life and the school has been our home. Our parents have given us support and encouragement. Teachers have gone out of their way to help us. Now we must take everything we have been taught and put it to use in the real world.

This day, besides making me think of the future, makes me reflect on the past. We have changed so much since our first day of school. We have developed interests, and formed friendships. We have seen both success and failure.

We are leaving a place of security and entering into areas of uncertainty. We have all worked so hard to get here, but now that it's here, we ask ourselves, "What next?" We still have many goals to meet and challenges to overcome.

1991 (Age 18 years)

Debra S. Lewis

LETTERS HOME FROM COLLEGE:

September 2, 1991

Dear Mom, Dad, Jen and Em-

It's about quarter to five on Monday now. I've written four letters and this makes five. Neither my roommate or I had to take placement exams so we've had most of the day free. Her boyfriend came and took us to Friendly's in South Hadley. It was nice. After that he drove us to Atkins—*a great place for fresh food, especially apples*—about fifteen min. away opposite S. Hadley. When we got back to the college we had to have our class picture. Then we went to the campus store where I wrote my first check! I bought a heavy duty sweatshirt, this professional looking stationery, a keychain for all my new keys (four), a card for Scott, and some thumb tacks. We also went to all the shops across the street at the Commons where I bought a few humor postcards. I thought I'd send them to friends so they have some mail first day of school. After that, we walked to the far end of campus and looked inside Kendall (nice pool) and squash courts (for Dad). From there, we walked on a road behind campus with all the professor's houses. We came on to campus from the other side. So we saw almost all the dorms and the lakes, etc. etc. My roommate will have a nice phone bill at the end of this month. Oh, when we went to Atkins, I bought some (apple) cider donuts which

Audra guaranteed me were great. I hope so because I haven't had much of an appetite. We also drove by the MHC golf course which is supposed to be very nice. I like my school a LOT:

   Mon. French. 10-10:50, Eng. 11-12:15, Dance 1-2:30
   Tues. French 10-10:50, Pol. 11-12:25, Econ. 2:30-3:45
   Wed. French 10-10:50, Eng. 11-12:15, Dance 1-2:30, Econ. 3-3:50
   Thurs. Pol. 11-12:15, 2:30-3:45
   Fri. French 10-10:50

The weather is definitely fall. This morn, I wore jeans and a flannel shirt but it warmed up this afternoon to the mid-70s and I was hot. So I'm in a t-shirt now. I can't wait until classes start so I have something to do and can get my mind off thinking about wanting to be home. Thanksgiving seems so far away. I hope Mom got back okay and didn't suffer too much for such a long trip. Again, I appreciate all her help. She'll be shocked to learn that my bed is made today. I also learned that Audra likes to study on the floor so I have to keep it fairly clean. We're going to go bargain shopping sometime for a rug. I'll also probably end up buying a cheapo bike eventually.
   XOXO Love, Berni

9/08/91

Dear Mom and Dad,

There's not a lot new to say, but I thought I'd write a little letter. I can't believe it's finally been a whole week. It seems so long. I have had some fun, but I still get sad.

I've met people who have the same problem. One girl is from Puerto Rico and her boyfriend goes to school in New York. One girl is from Oregon. But then there are many who live within four or five hours and those who went to boarding school. So some are more energetic than others. But I think I'm going to go see Rocky Horror Friday night. There's fun stuff like that. There's also dumb stuff like games for seven year olds. I'm just not in the mood for that. I'm eating a little more, but I still think I ate way more at home. The crew coach called my room when I didn't show up for the first meeting. I was like, no thanks. It was funny though, because Audra had answered and was saying "It's a boy! It's a boy!" Thinking it was Scott or something. I hope you guys can come up on family weekend, but I understand. Keep writing—Emily too.

All my love, Bern.

9/21/91

Dear Mom and Dad-

I just got back from our first Rugby scrimmage. I got to play on the better of the two sides from our team. There were a lot of experienced players pushing me where I needed to be. Amherst is a very good team—with a coach—so needless to say, we lost. But it was just for practice. In about forty minutes, I'm trying out for Shades of Expression- a theatre, vocal, and dance group. Obviously, I'm trying for the dance part. But competition is tough. At the activities fair Thursday night, I signed up for twelve different organizations! Most of them, however, are low commitment, sort of special interest groups. Some of which include: College Democrats, Amnesty International, H.A.R.M. (like PETA), Hunger for Life, Peace Project, and

Womenspeak (Women Stuff). *Later on I'll figure out what I can and cannot do. I've met a lot more people now. I don't like to have just one group of friends, so I tend to move from group to group. The weather is getting cooler. I love getting mail. I really appreciate all of your letters and packages and phone calls. I'm sorry I haven't written as often. Last night (Friday) I went to see the movie,* Truly Madly Deeply. *It was sooo excellent. I love British movies. It wasn't a comedy, it was a drama, but it was wonderful. HAPPY BIRTHDAY TO JEN AND DAD. Can't wait until Thanksgiving.*

Love, Bern.

12/02/91

Dear Fam,

I really have a lot of work to do, so this won't be more than a page. But, I am finding that I am not alone in how much I have to do. At least, I don't have any papers due before Christmas. My economics class was cancelled so I'm using the extra time to write a few letters. I signed up for J-term classes yesterday. I got the two I wanted (stained glass and CPR), but I stood in line for two hours and missed my French class. It snowed last night! I was so excited. Except it's not the fun, soft snow-it's hard and crusty but it sticks well. Today was cold and wet. I already told you that I'm getting a ride back home with Jen, so don't lose the directions. I hope you all are driving around happily in the new car and that Jenine is practicing her stick shift driving. Oh, I went and saw the Addams Family yesterday. It was pretty entertaining. Could you add to my stocking list a book of stamps? I think I just heard thunder and it's pouring rain. Yuck. I have to go make up a French test in about forty-five minutes. Say hi to everyone for me. Mom, your cookies are almost gone (I shared); how do you get them to stay so soft after days?

Love, Bern

Debra S. Lewis

Song of Bernadette

ON WRITING:

Before I could write or read, my mom would read to my sister and I. I remember her reading all of the Little House on the Prairie books to us, as well as Watership Down. Once I learned to read, books became my favorite possessions. At the age of eight years old, I was given my first diary. This was the moment my writing "career" began. I've always been encouraged by my parents to write creatively: stories, essays, and poems. At Thanksgiving and Christmas, my sister and I were asked to write an essay on a given topic related to the holiday. English was always one of my favorite topics in elementary school.

I think one of the problems in education is that a point is reached where the emphasis on creativity is switched to one of analysis and comparisons. The main focus of English classes becomes on grammar. I think all of this is necessary, but unfortunately, the system I grew up in doesn't pay enough attention to the development of creative thinking and to the production of new ideas. A high school student is no longer asked to imagine what life would be like on a newly discovered planet. Instead, he or she is asked to compare two literary characters or themes. I think many students lose interest in writing at this point and once the desire is gone, it is hard to develop talent and writing becomes a chore.

I have had the same struggle as a science major in college. So much time is spent emphasizing scientific principles and procedure that often the quality of the lab write-up is only considered secondary. It is also hard to remain creative when one's training requires an extensive amount of analysis.

As a writing assistant, one of my main goals is to help others see the joy and beauty in writing. There is no limit to the amount of feeling and expression that can be conveyed.

1992 (Age 19 years)

Song of Bernadette

My calloused fingers strum the strings of your heart

As I turn away and stare into the emptiness

To the sad tune of loneliness

Your feelings vibrate loudly, but mine—

They are a beat behind, lost in another song.

8/17/93 (Age 20 years)

Debra S. Lewis

HOW TO BE A CODEPENDENT:

*Care about everything and
everyone all the time
Love instead of being loved
Apologize often—for things that
aren't your fault especially
Stop your activities for someone else's*

HOW TO BE FREE:

*Rip off your pricetag and dance-
Lift your arms in the sky and pray-
Run in circles or squares or rectangles-
Know yourself
Cry
Believe in your dreams
Break the law
Swim underwater
Skip
Be unorganized
Walk the wide and crooked
(Undated College)*

Song of Bernadette

Debra S. Lewis

"SURVIVAL"

OVERLOOKED:

Like the word "the" written twice consecutively
Or a comb within a drawer of accessories

AND LOST

Like the memory of one's great-grandfather
Or the ability to do algabraic functions

THROWN AWAY

As a newspaper dated two months ago
Or an expired coupon

IN AGONY

As when falling out of love
Or losing your best friend

Not knowing that all will be okay
And then remaining alive

(Undated College Journal Entry)

Song of Bernadette

I CAN'T STOP THINKING

I wonder what he thinks
If I was special
If he liked my feel

I wonder what he thinks
Did he have a good time?
If he liked my feel
He would have called

Did he have a good time?
It was just a party
He would have called
Had it been more

It was just a party
He drank too much
Had it been more
Then I'd know his last name

He drank too much
But he held me so near
Then I'd know his last name
If it was a true embrace

But he held me so near
I can't stop thinking
If it was a true embrace
If I was special.

(Undated College Journal Entry)

Debra S. Lewis

THE EDGE BETWEEN SUMMER AND FALL

Pasted white moon
One canoe's path
Young calling loon
A silent cat bath.
Stars in the sky
Ever so bright
Not even a fly
Buzzes in sight.
Maybe a bird
Or even a snake
Is possibly heard
As noises they make.
The night is still
There is a breeze
And on a hill
Swaying are trees.
The night is warm
The air is crisp
The bees will swarm
The crickets will lisp.
The bare dusty ground
A blanket of leaves
There is no sound
As a spider weaves.

(Undated)

III. AUTUMN

LIVE YOUR LIFE

Free as a Butterfly

Butterflies flying
High in the sky
Loopedy-Looping
Free as a bird

Butterflies flying
Deep in the meadows
Playfully laughing
Just like a child

Butterflies flying
Through the forests
Landing on flowers
Busy as a bee

Flying freely
No cares in the world
Loopedy looping
Playfully Laughing
Landing on flowers.

(Undated)

Debra S. Lewis

AUTUMN

Autumn is a time of harvest. It is a rich mosaic of vivid colors and diverse textures, a time of cooling off, a time of preparation for dormancy. It is a short, transitional season that sometimes passes unnoticed until the winds and gales of the coming winter are upon us. It is a time of collecting as we store away the plenty that we have reaped during our summer months in preparation for future times of lack. Autumn can be a crunchy time. We grind the decaying remains of our leafy summer produce underfoot as we walk about in anticipation of colder months to come.

I have chosen to characterize the autumn of Berni's life as her post-college and professional years, from 1995 until 1999. Although a short season, it was a crunchy time of continued adjustment and discovery for my remarkable and courageous daughter.

After graduating from Mount Holyoke College in May 1995, Berni got a job at the National Institute of Health in Maryland as a research assistant. She was an idealist who wanted very much to make a difference in the world. She fretted aloud about injustices. She remained a feminist and was intolerant of sexism in any form. Her social conscience was well-developed. She was fascinated with science and the natural world, but also loved the idea of helping people. She saw her position as an assistant to an AIDS researcher as temporary; an interesting means to an end until she fulfilled her long-term dream of being accepted into the Peace Corps. She wanted to go to Africa.

Unfortunately, Berni's dream of serving in the Peace Corps was stymied when she learned that her history of asthma would be an impediment to her being accepted and placed in the program.

There was a great paradox in Berni's life during this time. Her day job in the lab was repetitive, structured, and required meticulous attention to detail. She was good at performing these routine tasks, and was liked and valued as an intelligent member of the research team. On the other hand, her personal life was often chaotic and lacking in structure and focus.

Berni had a microscopic view of the world. Little things in life that no one else could see could irritate her. There was often a difficult edge between her and me when she would come home on visits. I have a macroscopic view of most things and tend to look at the big picture. I tried to help her focus on the grand vision in her life, and frequently, I was only able to see fragmentation and self-doubt. Our reunions during this time were glorious at the beginning and quickly eroded into tension-filled days and mutual judgment. We would part in tears amid promises that the next visit would be easier.

Berni would sometimes express feelings of being unappreciated for her view of the world. Her home environment, which usually consisted of one room, was famously cluttered and messy. She hung on to everything and everyone with a firm grip and a reluctance to let go. It seemed everyone she met was a lifelong friend. She kept in touch with her friends often through letters and long-distance calls.

Family ties remained important to Berni during her time living on the East Coast. Living a great distance from her family of origin continued to pull on her heartstrings and she yearned to be with us more often than she was able. She bonded with her East Coast Lewis relatives: her Grancy and Grandpa Lewis, aunts, uncles, and cousins located in Mantoloking, New Jersey; Purcellville, Virginia; Springfield, Massachusetts; and Wolfboro, New Hampshire. She treasured her relationship with her little sister, Emily, and baby brother, Peter, whom she barely knew. She took on the role of doting aunt with them, and considered it her duty and delight to introduce them to as many of the wonders of the world as she could. It was important to her that she stay in touch from a distance with her maternal relatives: her Vetsch/Peterson grandparents, aunts, uncles, and cousins living in Minnesota and Colorado.

Song of Bernadette

Not long after starting work in the lab, Berni met and began seeing another brilliant research assistant, Su-hun Seo. Su-hun was a second-generation son of Korean immigrants, and had grown up in Kentucky, in a similar circumstance as Berni. Su-hun's father was also a physician in a small rural town, and he, too, was an academic standout.

Su-hun was so much more to Berni than a fellow intellectual budding scientist. He became the love of her life, and her pursuit of the relationship with him was consuming at times. She often remarked how much Su-hun's path had followed that of Jeff Lewis, her adoptive father. They had both attended Yale University and had even lived in the same dorm, Ezra Stiles! We, too, loved Su-hun the first time we met him. He was brilliant, creative, self-deprecating, and had a wonderful sense of humor. He was a free spirit who allowed Berni to begin to soar into places she had never before traveled. They enjoyed many adventures together, and especially loved to camp and go hiking.

Su-hun brought to the relationship many friends with whom Berni loved to spend time. She adopted them all.

Despite the many friends and family in her life, there remained an undercurrent of melancholia and pessimism in Berni, which was intertwined with her strong push forward toward finding her place in the world and her purpose in life.

After deciding against joining the Peace Corps, Berni deliberated and agonized about where she wanted to go to school for her postgraduate work. We, her parents, had relocated to Ashland, Wisconsin, on the south shore of Lake Superior, in 1995. She longed to live in closer proximity to her siblings. She briefly considered applying to UW-Madison. In the end, her ties to Su-hun and the East Coast won her over, and she made the decision in early 1996 to remain in Maryland.

In 1996, Berni moved to the Institute of Human Virology in Baltimore, a lab associated with the University of Maryland. Initially, she commuted by train from her apartment in Gaithersburg, Maryland, but moved to Baltimore in January of 1997. In October 1997, she left the field of HIV research and began working with a woman researcher, seeking a cure for breast cancer. Her job involved working with mice in the lab, as part of her study of mammary gland development. These were productive years for her, as she learned the discipline of holding down a job, living within her means, and cooking. The girl who left home barely knowing how to boil water had developed the rudimentary skills of gourmet cooking, thanks in large part to her time spent with her aunt Cindy. She began subscribing to *Martha Stewart Living* magazine, a move likely fueled by a strong yearning to make a home for herself.

Just as autumn fades quickly from brilliant foliage and harvest time, so too, the vibrant autumn colors of Berni's life faded in a flash into the bleakness of winter.

She died during the season of autumn, on October 24, 1999.

Song of Bernadette

AT NIGHT

When you look into the sky
Don't you wonder
What's out there for you?

If you do;
And you know;
Reach your dream
I'm saying do what you need to accomplish in life
And live it

1984 (Age 11 years)

SORROW IN THE FEAST

The leaves have all changed color and fallen to the ground. There is a frost in the air, the temperature has dropped and summer has changed to autumn.

The best part about this season is Thanksgiving. It is the feast that most people look forward to each year. It is a time to gather with family and friends. It is a time to give thanks for all the blessings we have been given, but also a time to remember the hungry. I, like many others, feel very fortunate on Thanksgiving Day.

It's sad to think that there is sorrow on a day when everything is supposed to be joyous. In some areas of the world, people are dying of starvation. Instead of feeling full and contented, they are hungry.

I hope that these people can be helped so that they too can give thanks for abundance. We should continue to care and give with our hearts.

1987 (Age 14 years)

1995:

Dear Mom and Dad,

I'm sorry it has taken me so long to write to you/send these gifts. Happy belated birthday (Mom) and Father's Day (Dad). I also sent Peter and Emily a package. The dinosaur stuff is for Pete, and I got Em something to entertain herself with in the driveway. Teach her how to play hopscotch for me. Maybe the box will come with a catalogue for you-it's great stuff. If you haven't sent the videotape of my graduation yet (or any extra pictures you may have—mine got exposed and turned out like caca) please do. I got rollerblades. There's a really nice bike path nearby, but since a good bike costs money and is a pain in the ass to transport, I thought rollerblades would be more practical (see Dad, college

DID teach me something). I'm still loving my job, except when it's slow and I don't have a lot to do. When I have something to do, time goes by fast—it's like being in lab at school except that the generated data is used for future experiments/papers. If it's convenient, could you look into getting a schedule of fall classes from the local community college for me? I'd also like one from the U of M if you get down to Mpls. this summer. Depending on if they're on semesters or trimesters, I figured I could get a start on the four courses I still need to take before applying to medical school. (2 chem, 2 physics) If I don't get accepted for this winter Peace Corps assignment (I've been really slow with my nomination packet form—I hate paperwork—and I haven't even received my medical forms yet), there will be plenty of programs—although probably for teaching biology and not in health extension—before leaving next summer. Then hopefully I could fulfill all of my requirements during the school year (2 classes/semester) and be ready to go when I got done with Peace Corps. Or I could do Teach for America or Lutheran Volunteer Corps which is only a one-year time commitment. I just want to do some type of social service program while I don't have any debts to pay off and only have to worry about sustaining myself for the short-term. Also, LVC would not be affected by any government budget cuts. I still can't decide if I want to go to med school or if I want to go to graduate school for science writing. I suppose, though, that if I'm doing medical research, that I'd be writing papers as well. Plus, there are always the weekends for writing—I really don't want the pressure of having to write as a career and in order to make money. It'd be a good thing to do while on maternity leave when I decide to have kids, but that's such a small fraction of my time. Well, I've rambled a whole bunch, and it's time for me to work now (my supervisor just got in), so I'll talk to you soon.

Love, Bern.

Update: Besides my allergies, I'm doing great! It has been SO hot and humid though, which sucks. I went and saw Pocahontas with Allie tonight. Worth seeing, but not Disney's greatest (too Hollywood). There are still a bunch of movies I want to see. Well, I should go to sleep now. I'm tired and have to get up early to pack for the shore tomorrow.

Debra S. Lewis

TO MY BEDROOM FLOOR:

I know you're a mess
And that's my fault
I guess I'm too lazy to move
So suffer awhile
Beneath the weight of
My clothes, my books, and
Other things
I'll relieve you of your
Burdens tomorrow

e-mail 4/30/96

I've been putting off telling you this, because I haven't wanted to disappoint you, but I've decided to stay here for awhile. I think I was just feeling rushed, and wasn't sure I wanted to go, which is why I wasn't doing anything. I am going to take a physics class this summer at NIH if they offer one, since they are only $200, meet at night, and don't require labs. So I'm thinking I'll stay here at least for the summer and we'll see after that. My supervisor may be here until September for how fast (SLOW) things seem to be moving along right now. Mark thinks that if I work another year in the lab that I'd be able to go anywhere, but right now, I'm not quite skilled enough, am still an RA-1 and would end up washing glassware in some U of W lab for $6/hr. Plus, I'm actually starting to have fun here. I don't mean to offend, but part of me also thinks that, after the way you guys have been hounding me about my future, being nearer to you may make our relationship worse. Anyway, I've decided to just tell you about what I'm doing as I do it so that I don't have to feel obligated to do anything I'm not sure I want to do. I know you hate my uncertainty, but I'm not ready to be settled like you are yet. My gel's ready.

Later, Bern

JOURNAL ENTRIES

9/11/96 (On Su-Hun)

I got back from a visit in Wisconsin last night, after six nights away from Su-Hun! I missed him, I ached at times, but I was sick most of the trip and so it was mostly okay being without him. Until this trip, I think we spent every single day since I got back from Boston with one another. I am afraid that he has become my everything. I don't like to think that I'm dependent on him, at least not for my most important needs; rather, I like to think that I am independent in the relationship, but dependent on the relationship. Meaning: I like the two of us being together. I like always being with him, but within that togetherness, I am my own person. I don't give in to his opinions, I dress how I want to dress, I don't act happy when I'm not, etc. Maybe it's not much of a distinction. Independence is good. It's true that some of my always wanting to be with him may be because I can right now and because I'm afraid, insecure, that it won't always be that way. I mean, that shouldn't be a big deal in the long run, but the thought of him being gone is super scary to me. I can say that after we've been apart, our "reunions" are spectacular.

11/03/96 (On Depression/Dying)

I can't sleep. You could say that I'm really sad. I keep thinking about how I don't have a single friend in the world; nobody to stand by me, no one who knows me anyway. The few who do know me aren't with me now and haven't been for awhile. I keep thinking about what people would say if tomorrow they found out that I was dead.

Work: She's been grumpy—just bad PMS or hunger pains.

Margaret (roommate): I never saw her anymore. I thought she was happy and in love.

Family:"We did what we could to help her"Friends: She seemed so well put together—her life was in order, good job, nice apt, boyfriend.

Su-Hun: I told her to get help. I couldn't help her. couldn't give her what she needed. I couldn't even love her, even though I wanted to. I liked her a lot, though.

1/23/97 (On Baltimore)

…I moved to Baltimore on 1/04/97 and this is my second night I've spent here, but it's the first night alone. The city is so noisy—sirens all the time, cars with loud stereos… and I'm a little scared. Not a lot, though—I'm exhausted and expect to sleep well…

3/27/97 (On the future)

I left work one hour ago so that I could study and I haven't started yet. But I HAVE to study every night until my test so that I thought I would start at 7, and then at 10, I'll let myself take a break to clean my room or read or something. Right now, I'm baking one of the beer breads that Mom and Dad sent me for my birthday. I'm so tired all the time. I'm really glad I've decided to take this Friday off. Hopefully, I'll be able to get at least six hours of studying done during the day. I really want to do well. I know I can do it... I just have to. I wish I knew what the future held and whether I'll get into medical school to make all this S--- worth it. At least I'll be out of debt pretty soon. (2-3 mos.)

8/03/97

...Su-Hun's in Montana with his parents. He left last night and I miss him already. It'll be sort of nice, though. I think I need a break. I need to do so many things and I need to do nothing. I'm going to try to find a place to live. I want to do some pleasure reading and some reading for class. I want to listen to music and clean my room, change my oil, restart my afghan, go grocery shopping, plan meals, cook, organize my coupons, my recipes, my sweaters. Plus I have a lot to do at work.

8/04/97

Yeah! I found a place to live—small, cozy, hardwood floors, gas heating, cheap rent ($225/mo.), 5 min. to work by foot, all women... And I can move in anytime...think I'll do so gradually after the 15*th*, before I leave for vacation on the 21*st*. Woo-hoo! Now I have to go through my stuff and get rid of the crap!! I also went to Fresh Fields—spent $70! But I made a yummy dinner, bought some fresh veggies (the nicest bell peppers I've seen in a long time), bought a zester, some dried mushrooms, sun-dried tomatoes, etc. I'm going to start packing my lunch. How boring my life must be—to write about food and grocery shopping.

12/15/97

I feel really positive right now, and hopeful. I haven't felt like this, like there are so many possibilities for the future, for awhile. I can imagine myself being so many things—not just a doctor—and I can imagine the same thing for Su-Hun. I also can imagine us together. With Su-Hun, I think this is my first <u>real</u> relationship. This is what it feels like to truly know and love and care for and be devoted to someone else. And I'm still ME. I love it! And I love him!

Debra S. Lewis

Christmas Letter December 1997

In January, I moved to Baltimore and cut my commute from an hour and a half by train to five minutes by foot. I am now living in my third residence in the city but I hope to stay here awhile. Thank God, I no longer live near the murder capital of the U.S.! (Baltimore has only the second highest crime rate in the country.) Actually, Baltimore is a very cool, blue-collar, down-to-earth city (rare on the east coast) and I encourage anyone to visit. I'll protect you with my pepper spray and we won't go near the eastern shore. (Pfisteria is big news here.)

I was recently featured on three broadcasts of the local news discussing my participation in a transgenic potato vaccine study for traveller's diarrhea caused by E. Coli. For this, I eat raw potatoes and poop in a cup.

I am in the middle of my third (of four) pre-req courses for medical school, which I take free at the University of MD as part of my job benefits. As a biology major, I didn't take enough chemistry or physics. I plan to take the MCATs in April and apply to medical school next summer.

In October, my boss of the past two years returned to Virginia to do research. I was sick of moving and found another key position and decided to stay at the Institute of Human Virology. I am now working for a woman researcher studying mammary gland development and breast cancer and a virus called SV40. I am still dating my super honey (Su-hun), who is now studying in Philadelphia for the year.

Debra S. Lewis

THE SEARCH FOR DOOM

As I look into the future
To see what I can see
I see peace
And love

To see what I can see-
It's not always fair
And love,
It's the hardest thing of all
When so many things are false

Tho' I search for truth
I find myself misled
When so many things are false
And I know I've been defeated

I find myself misled
I see peace
And I know I've been defeated
As I look into the future.

(Undated)

IV. WINTER

WE LIE IN OUR GRAVES

Her silence could be ironic
Had it come from admiration or boredom
Or any other emotion over which she had control.
She would never choose to be silent.
This eternal silence was completely natural and inevitable,
Yet, as I stood there looking at her perfectly positioned self—
the centerpiece—I couldn't help thinking of noisier times.

(Undated)

GONE

It slowly fades like a sunset does
As it walks across the sky; then sleeps
My heart is turned away, left sightless
Maybe to be seen another day

Maybe to be seen again
Or maybe left for eternity
Instead of rising early morn,
It sets, forever gone.

(Undated)

Debra S. Lewis

WINTER

Winter is a time of drawing inward, a time of dormancy as nature rests from the labors of production. In many ways, it is a time that reminds us of the sting of death, as well the sparkling promise of new life. We cover and put our flower and vegetable gardens to bed for a long winter's nap. We move more slowly during the winter and bundle ourselves against the elements. The days are shorter and the darkness longer. Sunlight seems scarce and fleeting. We close ourselves in, sheltering ourselves from the howling wind and the biting cold.

Winter is a time of renewal of the spirit within, a time of purity. We watch the snowflakes drifting to the ground, whitening the landscape and presenting it to us in renewed splendor. We notice the shapes of each individual flake, the brightness of a starlit sky, the sparkle of moonlight on a fresh-fallen snowfall. We see these tiny miracles, and they give us flashes of the coming spring in the midst of the bleakness and barrenness that surrounds us.

A few notable events occurred in the winter of Bernadette's life. During Bernadette's final year, she became comfortable with her decision to apply to medical school, and as a result, she developed a focus for her future path. She seemed more centered and less fearful and lonely.

Towards the end of her life, Berni also adopted an Alaskan malamute pup and named her Lola. Next to Su-hun, Lola was Berni's second love of her life. Lola was an extremely energetic (and badly behaved) dog that taxed the patience of most people—but not Berni. Berni structured her daily activities around Lola and loved Lola unconditionally, through thick and thin. She and Lola became well-known in and around the dog parks in inner-city Baltimore, where owners would bring their dogs for exercise and socialization.

Berni also began volunteering to go into schools and neighborhoods as an educator to teach teenagers in the inner city how to prevent HIV transmission. She received her training through a program at the University of Maryland. During her short tenure in the program, she made a difference in the lives of many people with whom she worked. We later learned that her passing had a profound impact not only on the young people she mentored but also among the community of her co-volunteers.

The last time I saw my daughter alive on this earth was in July 1999. Out of kindness, Berni offered to drive out from Baltimore with Lola and take care of Emily and Peter while Jeff and I went to Hawaii. She jumped at the opportunity to use her vacation time to bond with her little sister and brother for an extended period of time.

Following our return from Hawaii, she stayed with us for another week and then made plans to hike and camp alone with Lola on the North Country hiking trail on the north shore of Lake Superior. Berni made preparations for days for this trip. It was her intention to be on the trail for four days. After long hours of tedious preparation, making sure she had everything she needed, she set off. Despite our misgivings about her camping alone in the wild, she convinced us that the trip was necessary and important to her. As parents, we had to let go of trying to impose our wishes on her.

Bright and early the next morning, Berni returned to our house, frustrated and exhausted. Lola had misbehaved on the trail and had been uncontrollable, wreaking havoc on Berni's plans for a quiet time of solitude in the woods.

A few days later, Berni set off for Baltimore with Lola in her loaded-to-the-hilt Toyota Corolla, for a solo cross-country drive from our home in northern Wisconsin. Berni lingered and delayed her departure until the last possible moment. There was a feeling of heaviness and resignation as we said our good-byes amid thoughts about the long, lonely drive ahead of her. Had I known then that I would never see her again, I would have likely tried to hold on longer, or even driven back with her. None of us had any idea then about what lay ahead of us.

Bernadette's physical existence in this earthly life ended on the early morning Sunday hours of October 24, 1999. She had made the decision the previous year to apply to medical school. After completing her application process, the forms were put into the envelope and sealed. They were never mailed. Shortly after she completed her application, she invited several of her friends, as well as Su-hun's, to join her in celebration for a pre-Halloween pumpkin-carving party. The event was billed as B.Y.O.P. (bring your own pumpkin), and took place at the brownstone row house she shared with three other women in downtown Baltimore, near Camden Yards. By all reports, Berni was happier that night than many could remember having seen her. It was her last day on earth, and she made the most of it. She shared pictures of her family, told stories on herself, and danced with her dog, Lola. In a few short hours following, her work in this life was completed.

In the rush of her excitement to break out and celebrate, she convinced four other friends, not including Su-hun, to go the nearby railroad tracks with the idea of hopping on a slow-moving freight train for a short distance and then jumping off. After one failed first attempt to grab hold, Berni reached up and grabbed the bar of the freight boxcar as it passed slowly next to her. Almost immediately, she lost her grip and she was sucked beneath the train. She died instantly.

It is clear from her writings that Berni had pondered her own death and its impact upon those around her, as well as the existence of an afterlife. I doubt very much that she ever expected to die so young and so violently. It was her heart's desire to someday marry and have children.

I also doubt that she had any idea of the magnitude of the effect of her death on her circle of friends, family, and acquaintances. Were she able, in the days, months, and years following her passing, she would have witnessed what a difference one short life can make in the lives of so many others. Bernadette's short life and the tragedy of her death were like a small pebble dropped into a pond of water, where the ripples from the fall keep traveling further and further outward. One small, seemingly inconsequential pebble can stir movement that carries far and wide.

Her sweetness and sensitivity and compassion were signs for those around her of the love of God that dwelt within her. She feared and detested pain. Due in part to her great sensitivity, she had a low tolerance for pain. The manner of her death was a blessing to her and to us, as she did not have an opportunity to suffer.

Immediately upon her passing, she became immortalized—frozen forever like ice in winter: forever young, forever on the cusp of greatness, remembered forever by many for her generous, sweet, and free-spirited nature.

When we arrived in Baltimore the day following her death to claim our daughter, we were faced with an initial agonizing decision. We had to quickly decide whether we would bring Berni's shattered body home in a coffin or whether we wanted to have her cremated. After speaking with Su-hun, her one true love, and meeting with the undertaker, we decided that we would have her remains cremated. In the initial days, I was not ready to bury my daughter. Her free spirit could not possibly stay in the ground. We carried her ashes lovingly home with us in an urn.

We decided jointly with Su-hun that we would scatter her ashes in all the places that she loved the most. These included the beach at Mantoloking; near the dock at Rockywold-Deephaven Camp in Holderness, New Hampshire, where Berni vacationed as a child during the springtime of her life and worked during the college summer breaks; the Tidal Basin near the Jefferson Memorial in Washington, D.C.; the campus at Mount Holyoke, where she spent her coming-of-age time; the mountains and hiking trails where she hiked with Su-hun; and the neighborhood dog park in Baltimore near her last home in the autumn of her life. Su-hun also decided to take some of her ashes to the top of the mountains in Colorado, where he and Berni had intended to spend New Year's Eve in 1999 to welcome in the new millennium. We decided to scatter part of her ashes on the walking trail in Washburn, so that we could have a place of remembrance near our home.

Our place of remembrance is on the length of the walking path on the shore of Lake Superior, a place where I had walked with Berni and Lola during her last visit with us.

When I visited the place of remembrance the first time shortly after we had scattered her ashes in Wisconsin following her funeral service, I was greeted by a pure white seagull that was waiting for me atop of the sign at the entry to the walking path.

As I started my way on the path, the white gull flew ahead of me, as though leading the way. Some time later, I returned to the site to spend my lunchtime at my place of remembrance. There was, at the time, a bench situated close behind the sacred final resting place of my daughter. As I sat and ate, I became aware of a presence behind me. I turned and I saw a pure white gull, that sat silently at my shoulder during the time I sat and ate. Ordinarily, gulls are noisy and pesky and impatient. This gull was not interested in sharing my meal. It seemed to me that this gull was interested in being my companion.

I did not know then that the color of white is symbolic in the Native tradition of purity and wisdom, and that birds are often understood to be messengers of God.

The quiet presence of the white bird leading my way during that visit opened my eyes to the many respects Bernadette was ahead of us. Many of her qualities that drove us crazy during her life were not appreciated about her until she left us. Her life, like all of ours, mattered. It mattered that she was born, lived, and died on this earth.

Five and a half years later, another bird came to pay me a visit. As I sat writing about Berni's life and the lessons I learned from it,

I heard the persistent tune of a bird outside my window in the early morning, repetitively singing its song, the only song it knows. The tune was constant and sweet, like the primordial voice of the Creator, singing of love for me. I learned later that the bird I had heard was a male red cardinal. I also learned that in the Native tradition that red is the color of birth and new beginnings. I had come full circle. And now I was ready to move on into another spring.

Those of us who love Bernadette and desperately miss her wait the thawing of the ice and the melting away of the snows of winter. We welcome the prospect of the spring to come in the next cycle of our life together.

Debra S. Lewis

WHERE I CAME FROM:

The Land of 10,000 Lakes flows through me, except when it sometimes freezes. Not frozen from the cold, but from the distance. The cornfields of Ohio do that to me also. Still, it's only a three-hour flight to thaw myself. Then I become liquid and free, or I form into droplets and hold on to each solid object until gravity pulls me down into a puddle. There, if I freeze from the cold, I know it will only be until the next sunny day when I will become first a bubble, then a crack, and then explode again with my newfound freedom.

WHY MEDICINE?

Emily is nine years old now, reading books like Charlotte's Web and Little Women, though it seems it was not so long ago that I was reading Dr. Seuss books to her. My eyes still form tears of happiness remembering how I watched her sleep in her crib, her first time home outside of the womb, simply amazed that I had a new baby sister. I remember standing in the delivery room, watching in awe the sight of my mom giving birth. I saw birth not as a series of long contractions accompanied by loud screams, but as a beautiful replenishing act of creation. Emily's birth was the most

momentous event of my high school years, marked by feelings of immense joy.

Yet babies are born every hour, with the doctor's role in the delivery being all in a day's work. As such, the excitement of one particular birth is failed to be captured by the mere exclamation, "It's a girl!." One of the unique responsibilities of the physician is to be able to perform multiple deliveries, or treat multiple patients for the same ailment, while maintaining an individual connection with each involved. Aside from competence, I believe the most important skill of a physician is to be able to foster trust and develop a meaningful doctor-patient relationship she sees on even a casual basis. In fact, I see some of my strongest attributes as a future practitioner as my emotional responsiveness, my ability to listen to the needs of others, and my desire to attempt to reasonably satisfy their concerns.

These traits may be equally suited for social work or other ministry professions, so the critical question then becomes, "Why medicine?." As my experience has been varied enough to promote interest in a variety of disciplines, I cannot say what one event or exposure has led me to choose medicine as my ultimate path. My most obvious, and first, exposure to medicine was in growing up in a family of family practitioners. My dad, for a long time, was the only physician in a rural town in Ohio. As such, he achieved a certain fame, and I saw how much of a difference he made in others' quality of life. I also saw how tired he was after delivering a baby at 3 AM, or how disappointed he'd be if he had to miss a school recital. I learned from an early age that being a doctor required hard work and a strong commitment, but that the rewards could be great.

As I began to recognize my own talents, and to connect them with my love of science, I became more convinced of my own suitability for medicine. I then began to explore various methods of practicing medicine and to develop a broader understanding of health-related issues. During an internship at a public health clinic, I was introduced to the wide spectrum of professions involved in providing public health services. A subsequent internship allowed me to observe various care providers in their assessment and treatment of HIV+ patients.

Working for the past three years in clinical research has taught me how attempts at answers to unknown medical questions are made. Volunteering as a subject in research projects at NIH and the University of Maryland has kept me aware of patient expectations and needs. Finally, my most recent volunteer experience as a chaperone during gynecological exams and colposcopies has validated my own ideas for the type of care patients should expect.

My desire to be a doctor does not stem from one event, but from a combination of experiences which support this desire,

Debra S. Lewis

and from my strong belief that I, as a person, am well-suited for the profession. I know without doubt that nothing makes me happier, or generates in me more enthusiasm, than envisioning my future self as a successful practitioner of medicine.

1997 (Age 24 years)

JOURNAL ENTRIES:

3/98

Right now, I am so scared and feel so trapped and imagine failing or fear it and think it is such a struggle to be able to do what I want to do. How can it–the extremely intimidating/high pressure application process—be justified, when the real effort should be in measuring an individual's desire and suitability (PERSONALITY!) for medicine—it should be the #1 criteria. Yet, the scores matter so much more—it's amazing to me how many possibly really good future doctors can be lost this way.. I'm glad Morgan read my Tarot cards last weekend in NYC—I got a very "your future is brighter" type of reading. There was also what I would call a warning, about how I need to be careful not to give up/lose my individuality in the face of a strong pragmatic influence (Su Hun?). Or that I needn't be so practical/judgmental/rigid. Oh-cool thing- Lynn (from HMJF) is a ball girl for the Baltimore Orioles. I'm sooo jealous.

5/26/98

Valerie's been gone since Sunday (today is Tues evening) and it is so quiet. I love it!! I like Valerie fine and we get along fairly well, I just think I'm a much quieter, more private person than can be accommodated in this tiny house with two independent people. Su-hun's in KY and I miss him. I want so much to marry him and sometimes I wonder why we're not already. I know we keep saying it's because we have to get our careers straight first, but lately, I've been less and less concerned about that. A career will happen. I can make it happen—no matter what. But I'm not willing to compromise my relationship with Su-hun. It's too important to me. I also feel this need to plan out my life right now and marriage is part of that plan. I would love to get married next summer or maybe the summer after that would be better. Next summer, I want to hike the AT (Appalachian Trail) and then apply to grad school in the fall for entrance in the fall of 00. (So strange to think about the start of a new century; when I think about those born in the late 1800s and living until around 1950, I think they're ancient. I'm going to be one of those ancient people to the next generation.)

I'll also re-apply to med school next summer, assuming this April's scores completely sucked. (I haven't received them yet) and that I don't get in or don't end up applying this summer. Still, if I apply and re-take the MCAT in August, that's fine. By next April, when I want to start hiking, I should know whether I'm in or not. But if I don't apply, then I want to establish residency in WI and apply as a resident next year to UMD. As much as I want Su-hun to follow me, four years in med. school without him should be ok, since I expect to be crazy-busy. If I don't get in, then I want to get a PhD in biostatistics, for which I need to take some math courses this fall…at UMBC hopefully.

7/22/98

Another night of wasted study time—what is wrong with me?! I DID finish my book, A Walk in the Woods, though, which was quite satisfying. Work is completely draining. I can't wait until vacation! I plan to finish all my rat RNA extractions by Friday, begin the PCRs and membranes next week, and then not think about a single thing! I'm so tempted to take another week off, but really can't since Shaunte would then be all by herself. Besides, Minglin might want a little break. I so badly want to go part-time. I don't understand why Dr. F. said no, then she'd have to hire someone else, when Albot worked PT for over 3 years! I just find that I am always exhausted—trying to cram 10 hours of work into 8. I'm losing my drive and if Dr. F had any idea and cared, maybe P.T. would be a possibility. As nice as she is, as much as I admire the way she kicks ass, I don't want to be the type of doctor she is, I realize. Actually, one of my biggest fears in becoming a doctor is of gaining this attitude of overly self-importance that others work for you, not with you. Power truly is corrupting. So often people forget that they work with other people with their own interests, relationships, and intellectual curiosity. I think Dr. F. is so nice, but I also imagine that she has become something she didn't used to be that prevents her from really relating with people "below" her. Maybe I just feel underestimated—a horrible feeling, but one probably to be expected with my current position and education level. It kills me that it's completely feasible that Shaunte could occupy a position like mine—though obviously it'd be fulfilled differently in a year. But then, that's ME being condescending, isn't it?

5/01/99 (On Lola)

What a difference in mood having a dog makes! I want to remember Lola's "birthday," April 20—the day she went into heat. I have no idea how old she is—I took her home Dec.19th—the vet said about a year, I thought younger, but I'll pretend this was her first heat and that she's one. She's such a sweet dog—especially when she's sleeping.

Song of Bernadette

Debra S. Lewis

ON DEATH AND AFTERLIFE:

"Thus, that which is the most awful of evils, death, is nothing to us, since when we exist there isn't death and when there is death we don't exist."

This statement is simply stating the truth. To me, its meaning is that nobody can tell others what death is like because that person doesn't know. No one knows what death is like until she dies. By then, it's too late. There are many ways to imagine what death is like, but no one can say with absolute certainty. There is no actual proof that heaven and hell even exist. That information is based on belief or faith. I choose to believe in an afterlife, mainly because it sounds less depressing than nothing.

If there is no afterlife, I might be afraid of dying. It's hard for me to imagine not existing, either in body or soul. Life is competitive, confusing, and sometimes difficult. It's nice to think that after working hard and trying to make the best of yourself, that a time of peace comes. A forever time of relaxation.

It's just as hard for me to think of "nothing" after death as it is for me to think of eternity. Eternity is forever. Forever is a very long time. It can't be said in simpler terms. I'm not saying that I'm looking forward to death, but I'm saying that I don't fear death. It happens to all of us, and it can't be explained by any human being.

1990 Essay (Age 17 years)

Song of Bernadette

Debra S. Lewis

DO YOU EVER THINK ABOUT WHERE YOU WANT TO DIE?

>*I want to die in the shower. Just slip down and float gently down the drain. The next person who took a shower would send their dirt to pass over you. And you'd know that they were clean. And it would be a reminder that you, too, were once clean. But now you're dead.*
>
>(Undated College Journal)

Song of Bernadette

ON MOUNTAINS AND IMMORTALITY:

The rewards of perseverance are great. Only with perseverance can one reach the top. On top of mountains, above the imperfect world to which I've become so accustomed, I can be free. I feel so high and strong standing tall, breathing clean air, and surrounding myself with beauty. I am the looker, not the looked at; I am above what is below. Sometimes when I reach the top, with my pounding heart, I look down in amazement at how far I've come and I cry. This feeling is one of true satisfaction.

I have often said that when I'm old, after I've had my career and family, I will move to the mountains. I imagine myself becoming immortal, taking the power from the sky and the rocks, the wind and rain.

Debra S. Lewis

The mountains are my inspiration, but, unlike the mountains, I have the power to control my own actions; I can determine my own destiny.

Below, I struggle to find that same high. I climb through education, above ignorance, in search of knowledge that will satisfy me. I change. I debate. I distance myself from "the norm." As the cold melts and the numbness disappears, I find true happiness. Like the stream that renews me on my hike, returning from the mountains provides me with new energy. It changes my perspective and allows me to realize my own accomplishments.

1992 (Age 19 years)

Song of Bernadette

*Pain has been and grief enough
and bitterness and crying,
Sharp ways and stony ways I
think it was she trod,
But all there is to see now
is a white bird flying,
Whose blood-stained wings go
circling high-circling up to God.*

*Margaret Widdemer
(Recorded in Bernadette's journal)*

Epilogue: Song Of Bernadette

SONG OF SORROW

The Song of Sorrow is a tune that I first heard as a young child when my father left the family as a result of his alcoholism. I heard echoes of it again throughout my life during my experiences of divorce, serious illness, and a move away from my lifelong home.

On October 29, 1999, the Song of Sorrow blasted me with its dissonant melody and nearly silenced all the other music in my life. In the past seven years, the Song of Sorrow has receded, opening the way for a poignant symphony to appear that expresses the inexpressible sublime.

What are the principal elements that enabled me to not only survive the horrific experience of loss of a child—every parent's nightmare—but also survive it as a transformed person, utterly grateful for all that has transpired in my life, including the lessons learned as a result of the loss of my daughter?

Prior to October 24, 1999, I was a person who tried very hard to control outcomes in most aspects of my life. "Control" was something I thought I was good at doing. Then there came into my life the most uncontrollable event imaginable with the worst possible outcome imaginable. Control was no longer my friend.

In the days, weeks, and months following my loss, I made many decisions about my life. Because of the devastating and shattering nature of the experience, these decisions were relatively easy to make. I was vulnerable—smashed open like a pumpkin on the street—with the particles of my old life strewn haphazardly along with the seeds of my new life. Looking back, many of the decisions I was forced to make helped me in my healing. It was as though a big rock had fallen on my tough, rational brain and my hard, defensive shell in order to finally relieve me of what was truly unessential in my life.

Looking back, I realize that I could have chosen a different path toward healing than I did. There were times when I felt stuck in the process. I might easily have become permanently stuck in bitterness and despair, dying a slow death inside with a sick heart and spirit, had I not followed the path that I did. It is clear to me now that the process toward positive healing involved making several key decisions. I realize that they are tools that can be used in the midst of any of life's difficult challenges.

Book Two: Choices

Chapter 1

CHOOSING TO RETAIN FAITH IN A LOVING GOD

    I had always had a faith in God, and that faith had been tested many times previously. It was easy to keep the faith when things were going relatively well in my life. The experience of losing my daughter was the truest test—the mother of all tests—a test that was in league with Job's final test of giving up all that was most precious to him. Early on, I had to make a decision that despite my tragedy, I would still choose to believe in a loving presence in the world that I named God; that I believed I was in the palm of God's hands; and that no matter how painful the experience, I could call upon this source of strength and I would find strength sufficient for that moment.

    Even in this, the darkest journey of my soul, when I couldn't see the light, I had to consciously choose to believe that the light was still there. I was comforted and reminded of this choice during the early few days by the fact that the sun seemed to shine brighter and more intensely.

I looked up to the sunlight every time I left the house as a reminder that God's love is ever-present, even when momentarily covered by the clouds.

My faith in God was sorely tested following my loss when we first arrived in Baltimore. I wanted desperately to cradle my daughter's body in my arms and say good-bye to her physically. After hearing the news of her death, I couldn't wait to get to the funeral home where her body was being held. Shortly after our arrival, we met with the funeral home director and were told that my daughter's body was not suitable for viewing. We were strongly encouraged by him to choose not to view her remains. This news was devastating to me. Not only was I not able to say good-bye to Bernadette before her passing, because of the violent nature of her death, I was deprived of the opportunity to say good-bye to her physical remains. It seemed so unfair.

I learned since that saying good-bye happens in many different ways over a long period of time. I learned that I had no choice but to trust in the wisdom of the people God had placed in our lives to minister to us in our time of need. In retrospect, I do not regret my decision to trust in the guidance of this loving presence.

Chapter 2

CHOOSING TO NOT QUESTION THE WHY

Because of the nature and senselessness of Bernadette's passing, I judged that I would never find any earthly reason why she died so young at a time when her life was seemingly so full of promise. I judged it so unfair that her life was snatched away at a moment when she seemed to be on the cusp of something so good here on earth. But I knew intuitively that I would waste a lot of my energy trying to figure out rationally something that defied logic. So I made a decision that I was not going to spend my time on the dead-end road of why. Whenever I was tempted to wonder about why this had happened to me, a good person, and began to succumb to self-pity, I would remind myself that I would not know and understand the reason why during this earthly life. I could accept that as a fact.

Chapter 3

CHOOSING TO BE UPHELD BY THE OCEAN OF LOVE

Almost immediately upon receiving our tragic news, we began to experience what I later dubbed an "ocean of love" from those around us: friends, family, and strangers alike. The love came in powerful waves, and at first, it threatened to overwhelm the old giver and scorekeeper in me, who was far more comfortable giving than accepting love from others. Being vulnerable to receiving the love of others means that I am not in control. This was hard for me. It broke the old rules that I followed, that God loves a cheerful giver more than a sorrowful receiver.

The love came in small tangible ways: like the friends who came to our home the first night and sat with us and held us and prayed with us; like the family members who traveled to Baltimore to be present with us in the hotel as we made funeral arrangements for two funerals—one in Baltimore for Bernadette's friends, and one in our home area for our family and friends; hotel staff who presented us with guardian angel pins as a token of their compassion; the strangers in Baltimore who ministered to us and comforted us and provided support for the funeral; neighbors who cleaned our house and had a pot of chicken soup waiting for us when we arrived home from Baltimore. Love came to us in the form of flowers, cards, food, prayers offered, vigils kept, hugs, and music. It seemed as though the whole of creation was reaching out to us in love. It was an experience that I had never had before, and I chose to accept it without question.

Like the tides of the ocean, the waves continued long after the last funeral song was sung, leaving us gifts that we needed at the time we needed them for months and years afterwards. The tides of love sustained us and kept us from drowning. Rather than swim against them, I chose to accept them with a grateful heart as the gifts that they were.

Chapter 4

CHOOSING TO ALLOW THE GRIEF TO BE POURED OUT

Grieving is a very strange and foreign process. Most of us have no training or preparation for it. I had previously experienced grief in smaller doses. I had lost my father at a young age when my parents divorced. I had gone through a divorce after being in an abusive relationship for five years. I had experienced the loss of my health for a time. All of these experiences paled compared to losing someone who was so much a part of me.

The loss of my daughter initially produced large amounts of uncontrollable grief. Waves of grief would wash over me in seconds, seemingly out of nowhere. At first, the intensity of the feelings was frightening for me. I feared that I would be washed away in tears, that if I allowed myself to start crying, I would never stop, or that I was losing my mind. I remember one night during the first weeks, when I was lying in my bed at night, I was suddenly gripped with a foreboding dread that overcame me entirely. I felt as though I was suffocating. My heart was racing. I felt as though I was going to pass out. I wondered if I was going to die. I did not know that I was experiencing my first panic attack. Not wanting to die alone, I called out to my husband to come and be with me. He held me in his arms and reassured me.

As I began to be more comfortable with the strong sensation of grief and learned with experience that it would ebb and flow with time, I began to give myself permission to cry whenever and wherever I felt like it, without apology and without shame. I realized that there is no shame in grief over the loss of a loved one. I made a decision to allow myself to be vulnerable, even with strangers, and to not hold it in, to reach out and let others know when I needed to be listened to—and sometimes, that I needed to cry with them.

Expressing our grief creates discomfort in those around us, especially those who love us the most. Our culture is largely ignorant of and does not value the healing properties in the grieving process. The unspoken rule allows a short period of time to get oneself together and then the expectation is that we will get on with our lives—almost as though nothing important had happened. We seek equilibrium in people around us. We want to depend on their behaving in ways we expect. Our impatience with the grieving process in others is motivated more by our fear than our compassion for them. We want those who are grieving a great loss to get better so that we can feel safe.

Song of Bernadette

Following my loss, letting the grief pour out for as long as it took sometimes meant distancing and protecting myself from those people in my life who could not tolerate the timetable of my groanings of grief, due to their own personal discomfort. These were well-meaning people who gave spoken and unspoken messages to me that it was time to get on with my life. For me, it meant seeking out those people who were emotionally secure within themselves and accepted me on my timetable, no matter where I was emotionally.

Chapter 5

CHOOSING TO MAKE TIME AND SPACE FOR THE GRIEF PROCESS

I was fortunate that I was in a financial position to be able to take the first year off from work following my loss, in order to heal. My husband gently suggested taking leave from my work in the initial days, and I quickly jumped at the idea. I remember the night when I heard the news that Bernadette had died. I was sitting at my desk in my home office. I reached over to a pile of work files sitting on top of my desk, and I firmly picked them up and set them aside on the floor. I said to my pastor, who was sitting across from me: "I guess I won't need these anymore for a while." In that circumstance, it was easy to give up all the extra responsibilities and commitments in my life that I had thought could not survive without me. I retained only those involvements that fed me. I learned that many things could go on without me there to control and make sure they happened my way.

When immeasurable loss happened to me, there seemed to be no room in my life for the mundane. Its importance just melted away like wax melting on the side of a candle. In retrospect, taking the first year off was one of the most important things I did for myself in order to heal. It enabled me to rest, to absorb, and to reflect. It forced me into deeper communion with my Maker. It was a precious time that I will always be grateful I took. My home became my sacred space of safety where I was free to function at the level I felt most capable. Having the opportunity to spend large amounts of time at home in my sacred space was important for my healing.

As an adult, I had learned to be very self-reliant, especially with my emotions. During the months of my sabbatical, I was blessed to have the opportunity to work with a skilled grief counselor. Mostly, she listened to me pour out my heart without judgment. She held a mirror up to my efforts to rebuild the pieces of my life. It was important for my transformation that I had a guide with whom I could reflect upon my rebuilding process. Not everyone can have the opportunity I had to have access to professional counseling. However, we all can benefit from the gift of a listening ear that we trust to hold us gently during our times of transition and healing.

Chapter 6

CHOOSING TO BE TRANSFORMED

Transformation means to be re-formed from an old form into a new form. For me, this meant transformation of my attitudes about life and my relationships with others. After my loss, it was easy to see that my life had been shattered. I was vulnerable and open and bleeding inside at a deeper level than ever before. At some point, I saw my experience as an opportunity to let go of those things in my life that had previously paralyzed me and kept me from being a more complete and loving person.

The first thing that went was fear. I had lived my previous life in a fear-based mentality. Fear controlled my decisions and wasted many hours of my life. Now that the worst had happened to me, I received a gift of no longer having to be afraid of lesser things.

To a greater extent than I thought possible, I let go of judgments of those people around me, especially my family. No longer do I take our time together for granted, as though it will last forever. I express my love to my loved ones every time I speak with them, and I end my conversation with a verbal "I love you." I know that when their time on earth is finished, their faults and shortcomings will melt away just like Bernadette's did. I choose to look for and to see the loving presence in each person I encounter as much as possible.

The old Deb was anxious about being perfect, and had great difficulty with boundaries between work and home. It was difficult for me to relax. Because of the nature of my work, I encounter many people in desperate situations. I took on the problems of others and carried them into my private life, wasting precious time and energy trying to fix and control outcomes. I still work hard at my job, but now I trust the outcomes to the strength that comes not from me, but from my Higher Power. I made a decision to do my work in a new work setting where it was easier to have boundaries between home and work. This decision allowed me to be less spent during my times with my family, who deserved so much more from me than they were getting.

I am a better and more productive person because I am more at peace with myself knowing just how much in life is out of my control. Outcomes are out of my control. I can still work hard to do my best and produce fine work. What is different is that before, I could work my fingers to the bone and still worry about the outcomes. Now I know that I am called to do my best and that God will do the rest.

More than anything, when my life felt shattered following my loss, all the trivial stuff that I thought was so important just fell away around me. I had been so overwhelmed in my involvements that I barely had time to gasp for air and go to the bathroom. I had the mistaken belief that I was essential to those activities, and that they couldn't happen without me. I had a mistaken sense of my worth. I was forced to realize through this lesson that I was not as important as I thought I was, those other things would either go on without me or not, depending on whether or not others saw the importance of these activities and were willing to fill the vacuum caused by my absence.

Before my loss, I white-knuckled my life a lot. I feared letting go of outcomes and hung on tight to the illusion that I had control over things that I really didn't. Afterward, I learned to let go and follow in the path I was led. Toward the end of my sabbatical, I was spending time at the beach in Mantoloking, New Jersey, and struggling with what I wanted to do about my professional life. I had allowed myself to explore the possibility that I would be open to doing something entirely different. As a family lawyer, I deal with many painful situations; it is taxing work. The system of justice is set up in a way that is difficult for me as a woman of compassion to practice in ways that I would like. The structure and rules at times can be confining and difficult. I entertained the idea that perhaps I could do something easier.

Debra S. Lewis

As I sat on the beach, after spending time writing and wondering for many months, I decided I would let go of the decision and the outcome and put it out on the ocean and see what came back to me. What came back to me shortly after I returned to my home in Wisconsin was an invitation from my current law partner to join him in a new venture of putting a new office together, so that I could continue my practice of law in a new and supportive setting. It was an opportunity that I had not considered on my own. I hadn't even known it was available. In retrospect, I am grateful for having made the decision to accept the change in my work situation.

Chapter 7

CHOOSING TO TREAT MYSELF WITH GENTLENESS

I have always been hard on myself. I had two critical parents who instilled a critical voice and a striving for perfection. In my old life, there was no way that I would allow myself to lie in bed all day and do nothing. That would fall into the category of "lazy." I give myself a lot of negative messages for mistakes and shortcomings and imperfections and especially when I disappoint others. I still struggle in these areas. However, I have learned that treating myself gently is a choice. It is easier to see in others than in myself. When I hear my husband berating himself unmercifully, I am reminded of how brutal I can be to myself. Before, I would feel compelled to toe the line, to live by society's rules that say don't show your vulnerability. You stay strong, no matter what. You continue to white-knuckle your way through life the hard way.

Making the decision to treat myself with gentleness meant that I did not impose arbitrary and unnecessary deadlines on myself, especially about how much time passed before I had to be finished with the healing. I gave myself permission to take however long it took to heal—to not use other people's calendars. It meant getting enough rest. At first, I could never get enough. I wanted to stay in bed all the time, even though I wasn't sleeping much. It meant eating good, nutritious food in small amounts, as I was able. It meant forcing myself to walk outside in order to connect with the natural world, even if just for a short time. Gentleness is an attitude. Gentleness towards ourselves is a choice.

Chapter 8

CHOOSING TO HAVE COURAGE

Fear had dominated my life previously. I grew up in an environment of fear and uncertainty. I lived for five years in an abusive relationship. I experienced thyroid cancer at a young age. After Bernadette died, I was tempted to fall into despair and to give up all hope that the world was a good place where good things could happen. I doubted my ability to continue to live a life of hopefulness. It was hard for me to look ahead and see a future unclouded by fear of bad things. The antidote to fear is courage. Courage is a decision. It is a decision that we choose when we go against the odds. We follow what we know is right. We stand up in the face of great obstacles and we say to ourselves: "I don't know if I can do what I know is right to do, but I will try anyway." Sometimes, I see the fear monster ahead of me that threatens me like a fire-breathing dragon. I armor myself with faith that I am doing what

Debra S. Lewis

I know is right and that I have all that I need to persevere. Courage is a decision we can make in all situations.

Chapter 9

CHOOSING GRATITUDE

Gratitude is more than a feeling. Gratitude is an attitude I was exposed to prior to Bernadette's passing. I practiced it on occasion. It is a decision I make to focus on that with which I am blessed. I was blessed after Bernadette's passing with the realization of how precious those people who were left behind had become. I no longer take them for granted. I was surrounded by so much love that it was impossible *not* to feel blessed. I treasured and pondered these blessings for what they were. I held my family and friends as if in the palm of my hand. Acquisition of material things had never been very important before. Now it was even less so.

Feeling grateful is a choice. Lamenting what I don't have is also a choice. Listing on a regular basis those things in my life that continued to have value for me was an important reminder of the big picture. Gratitude extended to focusing on the good things that had happened in my life because of Bernadette's death: the increased closeness and love I felt for my loved ones; the supportive work environment where I could more comfortably carry out my calling to minister to people in crisis; my ability to see and appreciate the small miracles around me on a daily basis; the gift of my continued health; the gift of being able to survive; the gift of a renewed and deepened sense of connection to my Maker and the Source of all Strength; the gift of Bernadette's friends in my life, who ministered to us when we needed it the most.

I am grateful for the gift of my first grandchild, Gabriel Lewis Mosher, born two days before Bernadette's birthday, in the spring of the year 2004.

Chapter 10

CHOOSING TO ACCEPT THE GIFT OF TIME

Writing this book enabled me to focus on my grieving. It has been a slow-moving vehicle at times, and at times, it has been stalled in the ditch for extended periods. Before Bernadette's death, I tended to be an impatient person who liked to tie things up in packages and put bows on them in short order. I liked to get to the heart of the matter. There was a sense of efficiency in my work. With my grieving process, I learned that using the gift of the passage of time would help me. The phrase, "Time heals all wounds" was one that was repeated to me often in the early, painful days.

When I started the project of weaving a memoir of Bernadette's writings, I set an arbitrary deadline of one year. I wanted to tie up the pieces into a neat little bundle in my old, efficient manner. After a while, people around me who knew that I was working on this project had given up that I would complete it. They stopped asking me about it. Early on, a wise friend suggested letting it simmer for a while, to increase the flavor of the project. Choosing to let go of the deadlines but hang on to the dream of finishing was an important decision.

Even now, so many years later, there are still instances where I am struck out of the blue by an electric bolt of grief that causes the tears to surface. I choose to accept those times as visits from my daughter. It is clear—even with all I have learned and all I have shared about my grief—that I am not finished yet, but the road ahead appears navigable and manageable. Of that, I am certain.

PANTOUM

A red bird dying
The angels crying
A flock of geese
Together sleep

The angels crying
In agony
Together sleep
With peaceful dreams

In agony
We cry in pain
With peaceful dreams
We smile

We cry in pain
A flock of geese
We smile
A red bird dying

(Undated)

AFTERWORD

For some reason, I remember her shoes.

My niece, Bernadette, was wearing "flats" on the sunny spring morning when I drove her and my brother to the Minneapolis airport.

As they got out of the car and walked to the terminal, I saw her shoes, how she carried herself, and thought how "cool" and cosmopolitan she had become at twenty-six.

She was headed back home to Baltimore, and my brother to Denver, following the graduation and party of my mother from college in St. Cloud, Minnesota.

That morning was the last time I saw Bernadette. She made a round-trip drive from Baltimore to Minnesota and Wisconsin that summer, but I was somehow too busy to see her, although I did talk to her on the phone from my mother's house while she was en route.

She died in late October that year of 1999, when she fell under the wheels of a train near her townhouse in Baltimore's Ridgely Delights neighborhood.

She was the firstborn of my ten nieces and nephews. A couple years before 1999, she had graduated from Mt. Holyoke College in Massachusetts. At the time of her death, she had applied to medical schools and was working on medical research in Baltimore. You can still Google and find a study for which she was co-author in 1999.

She was the first of what we hoped would be many prides and joys. Being first did not diminish those who followed.

Dealing with her death was—and remains—the worst experience of my life.

In a roundabout effort to try and make sense of it all, I set out in the summer of 2000 to tour Kansas for two weeks to find the roots of my grandfather, Harry Peterson. I might have made the trip eventually in my life, but never so soon if Berni had not died.

What I found restored a measure of balance and hope.

I found a wealth of living relatives, and stories of others past, stretching back to Delaware and the 1600s and, somehow, to Sweden before that.

However, that is all its own separate story.

I knew that if the opportunity ever came my way, I would visit Berni's haunts in Baltimore.

My work at Baltimore's Convention Center ended at 5 PM today. I walked back to the Mt. Vernon Hotel to change clothes and set out to walk the 1.2 miles to Berni's last residence at 605 S. Paca Street.

The walk is pleasant enough, past the University of Maryland Medical Center, past Oriole Park at Camden Yards. In fact, Berni's last home was only three blocks from where baseball is played for eighty games every summer.

You would never know it. South Paca Street is such a quiet oasis, lined with trees, townhouses built to the edge of the sidewalk. A red brick, three-story walkup. Around the corner and a block distant is the dog park where Berni played with her dog. Two blocks away is the gas station. A block further is the pub, Pickles.

Six tenths of a mile further south is the 1300 block of Ridgely Avenue.

Three rusted railroad tracks make a crossing next to an abandoned warehouse.

Two blocks away is the relatively new M & T Bank Stadium where the Baltimore Ravens play football. In between lie acres of surface parking lots.

It is almost absurdly simple to visualize the scene late on a night in October 1999. A car of young people stops short of the railroad tracks on the right side of Ridgely. Berni and a friend get out and wait for a train to come by that is moving slowly enough to try and jump aboard.

The scene is so innocuous now. So ridiculously ordinary and benign.

I have sometimes encouraged the nieces and nephews to dream big and reach high.

Berni had always held a dream of riding the rails. That night, her dream exceeded her reach.

Standing in the middle of the middle track, I could feel the possibility of chasing the dream for no more than thirty feet before falling short. I could see the feet touching the ground, running to make it happen.

I saw the shoes.

Oddly, it was not as emotional at the tracks as I had thought it would be—as it had been when I set out from my hotel in the Mt. Vernon neighborhood.

I stood by on Ridgely for forty-five minutes thinking of this and that.

Although I had the sense that Berni was no longer at this scene, whether or not she had lingered for a time, I told her of the amazing stories I had been prompted to learn after she lost consciousness here. I told her I would rather have learned the stories later and in some other way.

I told her she had been the maid of honor at her sister's wedding, and was now an aunt. I told her another sister was now living in Madrid and she would never recognize the cool dude her brother has become.

I told her that her grandmother had had heart surgery a couple years ago but was now standing for election to the Minnesota legislature.

I told her we missed her, and that as long as we all lived, so would she. I told her that she may never have known how much Irish was in her blood, and related the Irish blessing:

> "May the road rise to meet you,
> May the wind be always at your back,
> May the sun shine warm upon your face,
> And the rain fall gentle on your fields.
> And, until we meet again, may God hold you
> In the palm of his hand."

The train that came by as I walked away had the most mournful whistle, heard for blocks away. I have heard that train's whistle on the plains of Kansas, next to the childhood home and presidential library of Dwight Eisenhower in Abilene, and next to the homestead where my grandfather was born in Jasper.

Written by Gary Peterson, brother of the author and uncle of Bernadette (October 2006).

ACKNOWLEDGMENTS

I owe a great deal to my beloved friends and family who stood by me and believed in my efforts to shape this book, and I want to offer them my heartfelt gratitude—especially: **Al Chechik**, who encouraged me not to rush the project; **Su-Hun Seo**, the adopted son of my heart, who supported the concept of the book and generously shared Berni's written work; **Marina Lachecki**, who generously took me under her wing and shared her wisdom and experience as my writing buddy and mentor; **Jane Silberstein** and **Pat Ondarko**, whose advice and feedback were invaluable; **the staff of the McCabe Center** in Duluth, Minnesota, who supported me and fed me during my finishing process; and my daughter, **Jen Mosher,** for her honest insight about her sister.

I am eternally grateful for the love and faithful support of my husband, **Jeffrey Lewis**, for backing this endeavor through the years and for his unending devotion and loyalty.

Finally, I praise the Creator for the gift of my daughter, Berni, and the legacy she left to all of us.

Royalties from the sale of this work will be given to the Bernadette C. Lewis Memorial Scholarship Fund at the University of Maryland. Readers who wish to do so may send donations to the fund at the following address: University of Maryland, Office of Development and Stewardship, University Relations, College Park, MD 20742.